Filled with
All the Fullness
of God

Filled with All the Fullness of God

An Introduction to Catholic Spirituality

Thomas McDermott, OP

B L O O M S B U R Y
LONDON · NEW DELHI · NEW YORK · SYDNEY

Bloomsbury T&T Clark

An imprint of Bloomsbury Publishing Plc

50 Bedford Square
London
WC1B 3DP
UK

1385 Broadway
New York
NY 10018
USA

www.bloomsbury.com

Bloomsbury is a registered trade mark of Bloomsbury Publishing Plc

First published 2013

© Thomas McDermott, OP 2013

British Library Cataloguing-in-Publication Data
A catalogue record for this books is available from the British Library.

ISBN: HB: 978-0-567-57176-2
PB: 978-0-567-34197-6
ePDF: 978-0-567-14133-0
epub: 978-0-567-47944-0

Library of Congress Cataloging-in-Publication Data
McDermott, OP, Thomas
Filled with all the Fullness of God: An Introduction to Catholic
Spirituality/Thomas McDermott, OP
p.cm
Includes bibliographic references and index.
ISBN 978-0-567-57176-2 (hardcover)
ISBN 978-0-567-34197-6 (paperback)
2012045678

Typeset by Newgen Imaging Systems Pvt Ltd, Chennai, India
Printed and bound in Great Britain

CONTENTS

Introduction

*I came that they may have life, and have it
abundantly. (Jn 10.10)*[1]

These words of Jesus are among the most overlooked in the entire
New Testament. Too often we mistakenly conceive of God as a taker
and not a giver despite the fact that Jesus went to his death saying,
"Greater love has no one but to lay down his life for his friends."
We are often afraid to approach God—or, to be more precise, of
allowing God to approach us—because we think he will take away
something of value and give nothing in return, at least in this life.
But earlier generations of Christians were not so mistaken. When
St Thomas Aquinas, the thirteenth-century Dominican luminary
regarded by many as the successor to St Paul and St Augustine,
taught that the goal of Christian spirituality is human flourishing,
he was echoing an older tradition. Human flourishing, understood
in the Christian sense, is the "abundant life" that Jesus speaks of
and it is meant to begin here and now in this life.

Many of us have probably given little thought to the way in
which we are called to flourish or, to use a more traditional idiom,
to become holy. We have been told that we should "imitate Christ"
but are somewhat unsure of what exactly that means and may have
the impression that Christianity is essentially an ethical code with
the possibility of reward in the next life. This book is an attempt to
retrieve the part of the Christian tradition that pertains to growth in
the Holy Spirit or, as it is often called today, spirituality. *Spirituality*
is a word that enjoys popularity although it is actually a venerable
word in Christianity with a respectable pedigree that can be traced
back to the first part of the fifth century when it meant simply a life
guided by the Holy Spirit. For the avoidance of doubt, in this book
spirituality is defined as a lived experience in which the relevant
truths of the Christian faith are applied to the guidance of men

and women toward their spiritual growth. When we use the word *mysticism* we are referring to a heightened awareness of God's immediate and transforming presence.[2]

No spirituality can endure unless it is founded on some assumed truths or common principles. Catholic spirituality is not ambivalent toward those revealed truths known as *doctrines*— admittedly a "feel-bad" word today that is reviled in many quarters but which is derived from the innocuous Latin word *doctrina* or teaching. The principal doctrines of the faith are the foundation on which Catholic spirituality arises in all its varied forms. The truths revealed by God, whether in Scripture or tradition, were never intended as neutral pieces of information but are for our liberation and transformation into gleaming images of the Image, Jesus Christ. Catholic spirituality is life-giving because it is a lived theology founded on truth.

The Catholic Church comprises many spiritualities from the eremitical lifestyle of the Carthusian monk to the Catholic Worker Movement and Marriage Encounter. But every kind of Catholic spirituality is founded on the same truths about God, the human person, and existence as definitively revealed by Jesus Christ and proposed anew to every generation in his Body, the Church. Therefore, a general knowledge of the truths which are relevant to growth in the Spirit is an essential first step. A caution: Knowledge of the truth is never meant to be academic in the sense of purely and coldly rational but rather a *love-knowledge* of the Beloved. Theology—thinking about God—should be done on our knees, that is, in conjunction with a loving relationship with him. The way to approach the truths of faith is through knowledge, love (of self, others, and God), and contemplation. When the second-century theologian St Irenaeus of Lyons wrote, "Our way of thinking is attuned to the Eucharist, and the Eucharist in turn confirms our way of thinking" he meant that his teaching came not only from hearing (as a young man he had heard the preaching of St Polycarp who was a disciple of the apostle John) but also from union with Christ as experienced in prayerful participation in the Eucharist.[3]

The Church does not claim to be the sole possessor of every truth. The Second Vatican Council (1962–65) acknowledged the possibility of the presence of elements of truth and holiness in other religions.[4] For Christians, however, Jesus Christ is fully "the way, the truth and the life" who reveals definitively what it means to be human as well as the truth about God. Jesus is the fullness of truth who came that all people "may have life, and have it abundantly."

The sources for this brief introduction to Catholic spirituality are Scripture, the writings of the Church Fathers, and the saints and mystics such as Aquinas and the fourteenth-century Dominican mystic St Catherine of Siena, whose spiritual thought is virtually unknown although she was proclaimed a Doctor of the Church more than 40 years ago. I have also made ample use of the *Catechism of the Catholic Church*, a rich repository of life-giving truths, as well as the works of contemporary spiritual writers.

I would like to thank the following people for their support during the time of writing this book: Fr Paul Rothschild, dean of students at Kenrick-Glennon Seminary in St Louis, Missouri; Fr Anthony Eze, Ph.D., of Bigard Memorial Seminary in Enugu, Nigeria; Fr Felix Obialo, Ph.D., of the Archdiocese of Ibadan in Nigeria; my sister Lesa McDermott, J.D., Prof. Pauline Nugent, CCVI; and my Dominican confreres Alfred Lopez, Donald Goergen and the late Aaron Arce.

⇧

I am a countryman, Lord,
who comes from the country of the world.
Teach me your city's ordered ways,
the courtesies and gracious manners of your court.
Remove from me the likeness of the world,
on which I had been modeling myself,
and make me like your citizens,
lest in their midst
I seem as one deformed.
And teach me too
the language that I do not know,
the language I began to hear
when I came out of Egypt,
but do not understand
because I had grown up in an alien land.
Teach me the language you speak with your sons and daughters,
and they with you,
and make me understand those little signs,
by which you give understanding hearts to know

what is your good, acceptable and perfect will.
William of Saint Thierry[5]

(AD 1137)

Notes

1   Scripture texts, unless otherwise indicated, are from the *Holy Bible, New Revised Standard Version with Apocrypha* (New York: Oxford University Press, 1983).

2   Cf. Bernard McGinn, "Mysticism," in *The New Westminster Dictionary of Christian Spirituality* (ed. Philip Sheldrake; Louisville, KY: Westminster John Knox Press, 2005), p. 19.

3   Irenaeus of Lyons, *Against Heresies*, 4, 18, 5; PG7/1, 1028. Quoted in the *Catechism of the Catholic Church* (Washington, DC: United States Catholic Conference, 2nd edn, 2000), 1327. Henceforth abbreviated CCC.

4   Second Vatican Council, Declaration on the Relation of the Church to Non-Christian Religions *Nostra aetate* (October 28, 1965), §2 in *Vatican Council II. The Conciliar and Post Conciliar Documents* (ed. Austin Flannery, OP; vol. 1; Northport, NY: Costello, 1975), p. 739.

5   William of Saint Thierry, "Meditation 4," in *On Contemplating God; Prayer; Meditations* (trans. Penelope Lawson, CSMV; Cistercian Fathers Series Number 3; Kalamazoo, MI: Cistercian Publications, 1970), p. 117.

1

Self-knowledge

Self knowledge is at the root of all
real religious knowledge.[1]
BLESSED JOHN HENRY NEWMAN

Truth, according to St Thomas Aquinas, is the conformity of thought with reality.[2] Correct knowledge of the truth is vital. If we have a wrong idea of what it means to be human, then chances are we will love wrongly ourselves, others, and even God. To have a wrong idea about God is worse and has led to man-made atrocities in history like the Holocaust and present-day terrorism. But to have a correct idea about oneself and God has been the basis of stupendous human flourishing as can be seen, for example, in the art and architecture of the medieval cathedrals in Europe.

The two most important truths, therefore, are the truth about the human person and the truth about God. What is the human person and does he or she have a purpose? If God exists, what is he like and what should be our relationship with him, if any? In the light of Revelation, these two truths are linked because the human person is made in the *image and likeness of God*. For this reason, St Augustine of Hippo could pray: "*Noverim te, noverim me*"—"May I know you so that I may know myself."[3] Ultimately, Jesus Christ reveals what it means to be human. He reveals us to ourselves.

The importance Jesus himself placed on the truth is reflected in his reply to Pilate: "For this I was born, and for this I came into the world, to testify to the truth" (Jn 18.37) and in his earlier proclamation of himself as "the way, and the truth, and the life"

(Jn 14.6). He calls the Holy Spirit the "Spirit of truth" (Jn 14.17) who comes to illumine and unite.

Who am I?

Christianity insists that we are creatures of a Creator who is a loving God. Modern society, on the other hand, proposes naturalistic and materialistic explanations about the human person: he or she is essentially a sophisticated version of the animal mind which simply evolved into what it is today. One difficulty with this theory is altruism: How can we explain the altruistic behavior of certain individuals down through the centuries who sacrificed their well-being for the sake of someone else—even a stranger or enemy? Nonetheless, some researchers are optimistic of discovering a materialistic explanation for one of the most unusual human characteristics.

There are, of course, other visible creatures of God besides human beings: animals, rocks, and plants, for example. But the human person is completely different from all others in one important aspect which is revealed in the opening chapter of Genesis: "Then God said, 'Let us make humankind in our image, according to our likeness'" (Gen. 1.26). The *imago Dei*, the truth that we were made in the image and likeness of God, is the fundamental truth of what a human being is. It may sound like a pious nothing, something we have heard since childhood, and respond with "So what?" But perhaps no other doctrine of Christianity goes against contemporary philosophy and sociology as abrasively as this one does. The fact is that many people today reject it, as Benedict XVI observes: "Today human beings seem to claim themselves as gods and want to transform the world excluding, putting aside or simply rejecting the Creator of the universe. Man no longer wants to be the image of God, but the image of himself; he declares himself autonomous, free, adult."[4]

But if we are not made in the image and likeness of God, then we are indeed little more than highly evolved primates. Several years ago it was reported that at a zoo in Amsterdam the exhibits of various primates were placed in the order of ascending intelligence with an actual man and woman in the last one. How did we lose faith in the venerable truth of *imago Dei*? Various contemporary philosophies have undermined belief in it by proposing that the human person is a self-constituting autonomous subject who has no relationship with God (if he even exists). It is also said that we are not made in the image of God but God is merely an image of ourselves that we have projected.

Certainly the starting point of any authentic Catholic spirituality is the acknowledgment that we human beings are, as Scripture attests, "made for a little while lower than the angels" (Heb. 2.7) prompting the Psalmist to praise God saying: "It was you who formed my inward parts; you knit me together in my mother's womb. I praise you, for I am fearfully and wonderfully made" (Ps. 139.13–14). When we lose sight of the preciousness of the human person we then tend to objectify others, to see them as commodities to be bought and sold—as has happened in the multibillion dollar pornography industry.

Most Scripture scholars today acknowledge that the *imago Dei* is the central theme in the biblical understanding of what it means to be a human person. Furthermore, it is the whole person—body and soul—which is created in the divine image and likeness. We are created not as isolated and self-sufficient automatons but as human beings meant to be in relation with others, to the rest of creation, and to God. We are relational and social beings, reflecting the inner life of the divine community known as the Blessed Trinity. The New Testament goes further and affirms that the created image of God in the human person is brought to perfection in the *imago Christi*, the image of Christ, by the Holy Spirit. In Christ is found total receptivity to the Father, the unending Yes to his *Abba*, and infinite humble self-giving.

Our creation in the divine image and likeness means—and this too flies in the face of so much modern thought—that the human person is not just a something but a *someone* who is capable of self-knowledge, self-possession, and of freely giving himself or herself to God and others and of entering in communion with them. In fact, we only attain self-fulfillment in the giving of ourselves to others and, ultimately, to God.

The Church Fathers made a useful distinction between *image* and *likeness*. *Image* refers to the soul's possession of the faculties of intellect and will—two divine attributes that God imparts only to human beings and angels. Unlike other material creatures, we can reflect on ourselves and our lives and we know that we know and our actions are not guided solely by instincts such as self-defense and procreation but by free-will and choice. *Likeness*, on the other hand, refers to our likeness to Christ's deified humanity which is diminished or altogether lost by those wrong choices borne out of defective knowledge and love which are known as sins. It is Christ who restores the divine likeness in the soul.

By their very nature, the intellect is oriented toward truth and the will toward the good. As St Augustine says, "Our hearts are restless until they rest in God."[5] Only God can completely satisfy our restless minds and hearts because only he is Supreme Truth and Supreme Good. Finite things and persons, as beautiful as they may be, ultimately leave us feeling incomplete and wondering, "Is this all there is?"

"Imago Dei . . . capax Dei"

For centuries great Christian theologians and saints like Augustine and the medieval Dominican St Thomas Aquinas have pondered, in the light of Revelation and prayer, the depths of meaning of *imago Dei*. In his treatise *On the Trinity*, Augustine says that the soul is the image of God "in that it is capable of him [*capax* Dei] and can participate in him."[6] In other words, the human person is created with a fundamental orientation to God *for the sake of communion with him and with others*. Of all God's creatures, the *Catechism* states, the human person alone is "called to share, by knowledge and love, in God's own life. It was for this end that he was created, and this is the fundamental reason for his dignity."[7]

Christianity affirms that our vocation is to *beatitude*—happiness, ecstasy. The New Testament speaks of this reality in several ways: the kingdom of God, the beatific vision, entering into God's rest, or God's joy. The *Catechism* states that "God created the world for the sake of communion with his divine life" and it is important to emphasize that this communion is meant to begin *here* and *now* and will be completed in the state of being known as heaven.[8] As we will see later, this communion can only take place through Christ and with one another.

Our communion with the divine life involves a progressive union of our intellects and wills with the divine intellect and will such that God shares with us his joy, beauty, goodness, and truth. The saints and mystics speak of our vocation as *union with God*. When we are united with God it necessarily means union with all those in whom he dwells and is united with. The state of complete union with God in heaven will unite us more closely to one another than even marriage and friendship do in this life. Marriage belongs exclusively to this age, as Jesus said: "For in the resurrection they neither marry nor are given in marriage" (Mt. 22.30).

Communion with the divine life is possible only for rational creatures, that is, human beings and angels. Because animals lack intellects and wills and operate only by their senses and instincts, they cannot participate in the divine life either in this life or the next. To imagine a beloved pet in heaven would be like inserting it in the midst of a symphony orchestra which is playing a rapturous piece of music that would simply be lost on it. Pets certainly participate in God's being or existence, but not in his divine life. This is not unjust because non-rational animate creatures can experience the fullness of their nature in the course of their physical lives. We will not miss our pets in heaven because God will infinitely satisfy all of our longings for what is true and good.

Soul and body

We have mentioned the word *soul* several times but what does it mean? Many people today, influenced unknowingly by the thought of the seventeenth-century French philosopher Descartes, think that the soul is the same as the mind, the self, or self-consciousness. But this is not the Christian understanding of the word. In Scripture, *soul* often refers to the whole person but it can also mean the innermost aspect of the human person, that part of us which is most like God, where the divine image and likeness is chiefly to be found. The soul signifies *the spiritual principle in the human person.* Following Aristotle, Aquinas says that the soul is the *form* of the body, the latter being the *matter.* By form is meant the principle in something that makes it a living thing. The soul is spirit and is in every part of the body and acts on every part of it to make it alive. It is wrong to think of the body as thinly coated all over by the soul, or the body as a sponge which is interpenetrated with the soul, or the soul shaped identically to the body because the soul is a spirit and has no limitation.[9] When the body dies, the soul continues its existence because, as Aquinas taught, it is a *subsistent* form—a form which has existence in itself.

"I am not my soul," said Aquinas. We are *ensouled* bodies in that the soul is part of the human person and the body is also a part, but neither one by itself is the whole. For centuries the Church has fought hard against the idea that "what is real in me is separate from matter"—a false belief that has resurfaced in "New Age" spirituality. In essence this is what St Dominic preached against so strenuously when he tried to win back the Albigensian heretics in the south of France. The union between body and soul is so close that the two constitute one being. In some mysterious way, human bodiliness is part of what it means to be created in the image and likeness of God because the body is essential to being human. We see this in the resurrection of Jesus in which he rose to new life with his body—scars and all. The body, of course, participates in the existence of God who is Supreme Being and who creates all things and maintains their existence. The human sexual drive manifests our desire for union with another and, ultimately, with God. Our intellects and wills reflect, in a finite way, God's own intellect and will. Our desire for fullness, meaning, and "connection" also mirrors God's divine desire to be in relationship with us.

The wound of sin

We have intentionally left the subject of sin to the end of this chapter. This arrangement is very Catholic. The classical Protestant position on the human person is that he or she is first and foremost a sinner. Catholicism, on the other hand, asserts that the human person is first and foremost made in the image and likeness of God and that sin has distorted or wounded the *imago Dei* but not totally destroyed it.

When we talk of sin we must distinguish between the sin at the origins (or "original sin") of the human race and our personal sins. The sin of our first parents Adam and Eve (names derived from the Hebrew words for "man" and "woman"), a willful disobedience to God's command and a desire to usurp his divinity, has left our bodies and souls weakened by suffering and mortality. We are born in a state of limitation. Aquinas identifies four wounds to the soul left by original sin which correspond to the four *cardinal* virtues: ignorance (prudence), malice (justice), weakness (fortitude), and concupiscence or the unruly desire for the satisfaction of the senses (temperance). Original sin is part of the explanation for our seeming inability to do what we know is right and the inevitability of death.

Personal sin, on the other hand, is what people usually mean by the word *sin*. The glossary of the *Catechism* describes it as "an offense against God as well as a fault against reason, truth, and right conscience. Sin is a deliberate thought, word, deed, or omission contrary to the eternal law of God." Personal sin is an effect of original sin. Sin darkens the mind so that we cannot clearly see the truth of something and it weakens the will so that, in the words of St Paul, "I do not do what I want, but I do the very thing I hate" (Rom. 7.15). The doctrine of the Immaculate Conception affirms that the Virgin Mary was conceived without original sin and therefore was incapable of committing personal sin.

It is important to keep in mind that the one who commits sin is always affected by it. Sin shrinks the humanity of the sinner because it is contrary to our true nature, made as we are in the image and likeness of God. St Catherine of Siena says that sin is not only a rebellion against God but a rebellion against ourselves.[10] We commit sin, she says, because of our defective knowledge and disordered desires. We fail to see the truth about ourselves, about God, and about the effect of the sin we are considering. We choose sin because it looks good, that is, it looks like it will make us happy. But what we are seeing, Catherine says, is actually only cheap glitter sprinkled on top of something that is inimical to our true selves. "Sin is loving what God hates and hating what God loves."[11] The fundamental sin, she says, is selfish self-love.

It needs to be said that Christianity is emphatically not a list of "thou shalt nots" but is rather a loving relationship with God, as Benedict XVI reminds us: "Christianity, Catholicism isn't a collection of prohibitions: it's a positive option. . . . We've heard so much about what is not allowed that now it's time to say: we have positive ideas to offer."[12] Of course there are moral norms such as the Ten Commandments but Christianity is much more than this, just as a happy marriage means much more than simply, "Thou shalt not commit adultery."

Our thoughts and actions can be influenced by the Holy Spirit or by our own fallen human spirit, or by the diabolic spirit called

Satan or the devil. The Church teaches that the devil is a fallen angel or pure spirit and is therefore a creature of God and not in any way a rival. God never allows him to directly interfere with our free will but we are free to say Yes to his seductions. Not every temptation comes from the devil and it is wise to first look for a natural explanation of our wrong choices. The devil wants us to think more about him than God. "It is a mystery," the *Catechism* says, "that providence should permit diabolical activity, but 'we know that in everything God works for good with those who love him.'"[13]

No sin is greater than God's grace. Of Judas' two sins, betrayal of the Lord, and the taking of his own life, Catherine says that by far the more serious was the latter because he despaired in thinking that his sin was greater than God's mercy.[14] Forgiveness is always possible. "Is God not more ready to forgive than we are to sin?," she asks.[15] While it is true that grace leaves the soul when a serious sin is committed, God never washes his hands of us as the thirteenth-century Dominican mystic Meister Eckhart notes: "Man goes far away or near but God never goes far-off; he is always standing close at hand, and even if he cannot stay within he goes no further than the door."[16]

🕮

Nothing is more practical than finding God, that is, than falling in love in a quite absolute, final way. What you are in love with, what seizes your imagination will affect everything. It will decide what will get you out of bed in the mornings, what you will do with your evenings, how you spend your weekends, what you read, who you know, what breaks your heart, and what amazes you with joy and gratitude. Fall in love, stay in love, and it will decide everything.

-Fr Pedro Arrupe, SJ

Notes

1   John Henry Newman, "Sermon 4: 'Secret Faults,'" in *Parochial and Plain Sermons I* (London: Rivington, 1879), p. 42.

2 See Thomas Aquinas, *Summa Theologiae*, I, q. 16, a. 2 in *Summa Theologica* (trans. Fathers of the English Dominican Province; New York: Benziger, 1947–48). Henceforth abbreviated *ST*.

3 See Augustine of Hippo, *Soliloquies*, Book 2, 1 in Saint Augustine, *Soliloquies. Augustine's Interior Dialogue*. (The Augustine Series; trans. and notes by Kim Paffenroth; Hyde Park: New City Press, 2000), p. 55.

4 Pope Benedict XVI, Angelus (May 31, 2009) at the Holy See, www.vatican.va.

5 Augustine of Hippo, *Confessions*, Book 1, I in Augustine of Hippo, *The Confessions of St. Augustine* (trans. F. J. Sheed; New York: Sheed & Ward, 1957), p. 3.

6 Augustine of Hippo, *On the Trinity*, Book 14:11 in Saint Augustine, *On the Trinity (De Trinitate)*. (The Works of Saint Augustine; intro., trans., and notes by Edmund Hill, OP; Hyde Park: New City Press, 2007), p. 379.

7 CCC, 356.

8 CCC, 760.

9 F. J. Sheed, *Theology and Sanity* (London: Sheed and Ward, 1978), p. 105.

10 *Catherine of Siena. The Dialogue* (trans. and intro. Suzanne Noffke, OP; The Classics of Western Spirituality; New York and Mahwah: Paulist Press, 1980), ch. 21, p. 58.

11 Letter T29 in Catherine of Siena, *The Letters of Catherine of Siena*, (vol. 1, trans. Suzanne Noffke, OP; Tempe, AZ: Arizona Center for Medieval and Renaissance Studies, 2000), p. 207. Henceforth abbreviated as *The Letters*.

12 *Der Spiegel*, August 14, 2006, p. 56.

13 CCC, 395.

14 Catherine of Siena, *Dialogue* (trans. Noffke), ch. 37, p. 39.

15 Letter T178 in Catherine of Siena, *The Letters* (vol. 4, trans. Noffke), p. 263.

16 According to Eckhart scholar Richard Woods, OP, this is a translation of Sermon 104 in the critical edition of Eckhart's works edited by George Steer. I have not seen it.

2

Knowledge of God

If you think you understand God it is not God.[1]
ST AUGUSTINE OF HIPPO

Deep in the heart of every person there is a longing for something more. Even the wealthiest people never seem to have everything they want and, like the rest of us, are disturbed by a restless desire for a "connection" that will make them whole. The fact is that no created thing or person can ever completely satisfy us and make us fully happy. Only something greater than ourselves can do this and the only thing greater than ourselves is God himself. Catherine of Siena records in her spiritual masterpiece the *Dialogue* the time the eternal Father said to her: "People have been set above all other created things, not created things above people, nor can people be satisfied or content except in what is greater than they. But there is nothing greater than they except I myself, God eternal, and therefore only I can satisfy them."[2]

Our search for happiness, which many times leads us to the wrong places, is—usually without our knowing it—an implicit search for God who is Supreme Truth, Beauty, Goodness, and Joy. The Psalmist gives expression to this desire: "As a deer longs for flowing streams, so my soul longs for you, O God."[3] God is never passive or indifferent because it is he who first goes in search of us as shown in the parable of the good shepherd who looks for the one lost sheep. Aquinas says that our desire for God is a vestige or imprint of God's own desire or thirst to be in relationship with us. God thirsts so that we may thirst for him. The Fathers interpreted

Christ's dying words on the Cross, "I thirst," to mean, "I thirst for souls" which is to say, "I thirst to be in relationship with you." Desire, then, is written by God on the human heart at the moment of our creation. C. S. Lewis argues that our desire for God is a proof of his existence: "Creatures are not born with desires unless satisfaction for these desires exists. A baby feels hunger; well, there is such a thing as food. A duckling wants to swim; well, there is such a thing as water. Men feel sexual desire; well, there is such a thing as sex. If I find in myself a desire which no experience in this world can satisfy, the most probable explanation is that I was made for another world."[4]

Created for union with God

Like an artisan, God has left the thumbprint of his own divine desire on his human creatures as an impetus for us to search for him. Union with God is the goal, the end, the purpose of life. Union with him in this life can only be partial but it is, nonetheless, real. Allusions to union with God are found in Scripture, particularly in the Johannine literature where the words "abide" and "dwell" appear. In Jn 15, for example, Jesus urges us to remain united with him as a branch is joined to the vine. "The soul," says the great sixteenth-century Spanish mystic St John of the Cross, "lives with that driving force of a fathomless desire for union with God."[5]

But how can finite creatures who consist of matter and spirit ever hope to attain union with God who is above all creatures, self-existing, infinite perfect Spirit who is eternal, all-good, all-knowing, all-present, and all-powerful? That may not sound like an insurmountable problem to some people today who, having domesticated God and projected onto him their own faces, regard him as little more than a larger version of themselves. The sense of God's absolute otherness and transcendence is often overlooked. Years ago, altar frontals sometimes had embroidered on them the words *Deus absconditus*—the hidden God. The Eastern Church has done better in preserving a sense of the utter otherness of God when considered comprehensively as the Godhead or Trinity. Eastern writers, influenced by St Gregory of Nyssa's classic work *The Life of Moses*, say that the soul moves from the light of the burning bush toward "the darkness of incomprehensibility" represented by the darkness of Sinai. The darkness is God, Vladimir Lossky says, "for God makes His dwelling there where our understanding and our concepts can gain no admittance."[6]

The theological way of encountering God in darkness is known as *apophatic* or negative theology because it proceeds by negations: saying what God is *not*, for example, "God cannot be seen." The theological way most of us are familiar with is that of the *cataphatic* or positive theology which proceeds instead by affirmations such as "God is love." Both ways, however, are necessary. The Catholic Church, although it has emphasized the cataphatic way, has never lost sight of the apophatic approach as can be seen most clearly in the anonymous fourteenth spiritual classic *The Cloud of the Unknowing* and the works of Meister Eckhart.

We should, of course, always keep in mind the ineffable and apophatic nature of God lest we attempt to re-create him in our image and likeness and thereby into a god who always agrees with us and who can be manipulated. There is indeed an infinite chasm between ourselves and God which, seen from our side, is insuperable. The Fourth Lateran Council in 1215 solemnly proclaimed that "however great the similarity that may be established between Creator and creature, the dissimilarity between them is always greater." Aquinas, in his *Summa Theologiae*, (Summary of Theology) says that what "God is not is clearer to us than what He is. Therefore similitudes drawn from things farthest away from God form within us a truer estimate that God is above whatsoever we may say or think of him."[7]

Compounding the seemingly impossible goal of union with God is the fact that the *imago Dei* planted lovingly in us by our Creator has been disfigured—but not destroyed—by sin so that our intellects often fail to see the truth and our wills do not always choose what is truly good.

God intervenes

God acts, he intervenes, he takes the initiative—as he always does. He becomes a human being while remaining God. This is the great moment of the *Incarnation*—the enfleshment of God. Although hinted at in certain books of the Old Testament, particularly in Isaiah, few if any were expecting that God himself would come as the long-expected Messiah or Anointed One. St Catherine, having deeply assimilated the truth of the mystery, interprets God's action in this way: "Therefore, so that I might see and know you in myself and thus have perfect knowledge of you, you made yourself one with us by descending from your Godhead's great exaltedness to the very lowliness of our humanity's clay. So that I, then, with my littleness, would be able to see your greatness, you made yourself a little one, wrapping up the greatness of your Godhead in the littleness of our humanity. Thus you were revealed to us in the Word, your only begotten Son."[8]

The Jesus story is the astonishing account of the time when almighty God, creator of heaven and earth, became one of his own creatures knowing fully that they would kill him. In this most mysterious of all divine acts we glimpse the profundity of God's radical, self-sacrificing love. The momentous significance of the Incarnation was not lost on the English writer Dorothy Sayers: "Jesus Bar-Joseph, the carpenter of Nazareth, was in fact and in truth, and in the most exact and literal sense of the words, the God 'by whom all things were made.' His body and brain were those of a common man; his personality was the personality of God, so far as that personality could be expressed in human terms. He was not a kind of demon pretending to be human; he was in every respect a genuine living man. He was not merely a man so good as to be 'like God'; he was God. . . . Now, we may call that doctrine exhilarating, or we may call it devastating; we may call it revelation, or we may call it rubbish; but if we call it dull, then words have no meaning at all. That God should play the tyrant over man is a dismal story of unrelieved oppression; that man should play the tyrant over man is the usual dreary record of human futility; but that man should play the tyrant over God, find him a better man than himself, is an astonishing drama indeed."[9]

Jesus Christ is the ultimate and definitive revelation of God. He is, as Benedict XVI is fond of saying, "the human face of God." The New Testament speaks of him as Son, Word, and Image. To say that Jesus is God's Son is in no way a diminution of his divinity because each of the three divine Persons, Father, Son, and Spirit, is God. It is unfortunate that even Christians are sometimes ignorant of the full divinity of Christ, thinking that the expression "Son of God" means that he was only very close to God or very God-like. Every time we make the sign of the Cross, we affirm our belief that the Son of God is God.

Reasons for the Incarnation

Did there have to be an Incarnation? Was it necessary for God to become one of us? No. God is absolutely free and sovereign and could have decided to save us in some other way—or not to save us at all. Medieval theologians speculated that even a drop of Christ's blood or sweat or a simple divine nod would have sufficed to save us. But God chose to save us, that is, bring us into communion with his divine life, through his Son and because God is Wisdom itself, the Incarnation must have been the very best way. Aquinas thought it not unreasonable to think that any of the divine Persons could have assumed human nature but that it was fitting that the Son became incarnate.[10]

Theologians have long speculated as to the reasons for the Incarnation. The four reasons commonly given are summarized in the *Catechism* (457–60). Many of us are familiar with the first three but ignorant of the fourth reason—which is the most important.

First, the Word became flesh "*in order to save us by reconciling us with God.*" This reason pertains to the doctrine of atonement, a word that means to be in harmony or to be "at-one" with someone. Sin, as we have said, wounded the *imago Dei* in each of us, rupturing God's intended relationship with us as it had previously existed in the Garden. Humanity is therefore in need of healing and reconciliation, of *at-one-ment* with God. Over the course of centuries various explanations or theories have been put forward of how humanity has been reconciled with God. The ransom theory, which is one of the oldest, teaches that Christ's death was a ransom or payment made to the devil so that he would release the human race which had been enslaved since the fall of Adam and Eve. Another explanation, which is still current, traces its origins in part to St Anselm, an eleventh-century English theologian who said that Adam and Eve's sin was an infinite offence against God for which only a perfect God-Man could ever make restitution. It is worth noting, however, that no single explanation has ever been definitively approved because the Church has always recognized the inadequacy of any explanation. No matter what metaphor is used, the death of Christ did indeed reconcile humanity with God. While this healing has now been brought about by Jesus for all people, it must be subjectively appropriated by the individual. Catherine of Siena regarded sin as an obstacle, like a physical barrier, which stood between two lovers and prevented their total embrace or union with each other. But simply removing the obstacle, as necessary as it is, is not the ultimate reason for the Incarnation.

Second, the Word became flesh so that "*we might know God's love.*" The birth of Jesus Christ, the God-Man, and his horrendous death on the Cross, attest to the unfathomable love of God which could only be dimly glimpsed in the pages of the Old Testament. God the Father did not sadistically push his Son out of heaven and onto a Cross. Rather, all three Persons of the Trinity were present in the Incarnation and in the paschal mystery of Christ's suffering, death, and resurrection. God came himself and died for us. As hard as life can be at times, it is surely a consolation to know that God "took his own medicine" by becoming one of us.

Third, the Word became flesh "*to be our model of holiness*" or, to put it in another way, to show us how to be truly human. Through his teachings and actions, Christ shows us how life ought to be lived. However, we need to keep in mind that Christianity is not essentially an ethical or moral code meant to produce nice people.

Fourth, the Word became flesh so that we "*may become participants of the divine nature*" (2 Pt 1.4). Here, at last, we have arrived at the ultimate reason for the Incarnation: to make human beings divine, God-like, not by nature but by *participation* in the divinity of Jesus Christ. This is the doctrine of deification or divinization of which we will say more later.

The four reasons for the Incarnation illustrate the meaning of Christ's words, "I am the way, and the truth, and the life" (Jn 14.6). Jesus Christ, through his words and actions, shows us the way to be fully human; he reveals to us the truth about God's immense love and the dignity as well as the frailty of the human person; he is the life insofar as he heals us of sin and has come to share his divine life with us. The first three reasons are, in effect, means to the end of making us "partakers of the divine nature." Yet it must be admitted that this fourth reason is the one we have probably heard the least about. All of us have heard countless homilies on the forgiveness of sins, the love of God, and the importance of imitating Christ in our behavior but, sadly, seldom do we hear of our call to participate in God's divine nature. Note, once again, that this participation begins here and now *in this life* and comes to complete fruition in heaven. It is not something you have to wait until death to experience, as the Church attests to in the canonization of men and women as saints.

It is interesting to note how often the *Catechism* refers to our ultimate end or purpose as communion with the Trinity, the divine life, or beatitude and uses the word *heaven* less than one might expect. Heaven, in the minds of some people, is something one has to wait for and therefore it may not appear relevant to the here and now. On the other hand, the notion of divine life, of being fully alive, is appealing. Christianity is not just about "going to heaven" but about participating in the divine life, being in communion with the Trinity, at this very moment.

Sharing in the divine life

Jesus Christ, because he is God, is the fullness of divine life and became like us in order to share it with us. In one of the most overlooked passages of the New Testament, Jesus says: "I came that they may have life, and have it abundantly" (Jn 10.10). What an injustice it is to think that Christ came to take away and not give life!

But how do we puny human beings participate in Christ's divine life? We do so through the conduit of his humanity—the same humanity, albeit without sin, that we have. The more we allow the Holy Spirit to conform us to the humanity of Christ, the more Christ infuses us with his divinity. It is as if Christ were to say to us, "All that is mine is yours" (Lk. 15.31). David Meconi, SJ, is correct when he says that the human person is most human and only truly human when he or she is partaking of divinity.[11] The communication of divine life would be impossible if Christ was not "true God and true man" as we profess in the Nicene-Constantinopolitan Creed every Sunday at Mass. His humanity, and our own, is the Trinity's instrument for conferring the divine life on men and women.[12] Tertullian famously said, "The flesh is the hinge of salvation."[13]

It is important to note that our humanity must be *disposed* or open to receiving such a tremendous gift. Just being human is not enough. We must strive, with God's help, to allow the Spirit to conform our minds and hearts to Christ's as we come to know him in the Church, Scripture, prayer, the sacraments, and in our human relationships. What are the human characteristics of Jesus that we should aspire to? The *Catechism* says that "the Beatitudes depict the countenance of Jesus Christ."[14] Another way in which we can consider his human characteristics is in St Paul's great hymn to love in 1 Cor. 13.4–7 in which he describes what love is. If we substitute the name of Jesus where the word *love* appears in the text it may give us a different perspective on his human character: "Jesus is patient; Jesus is kind; Jesus is not jealous, he does not put on airs, he is not snobbish. Jesus is never rude, he is not self-seeking, he is not prone to anger, neither does he brood over injuries. Jesus does not rejoice in what is wrong but rejoices with the truth. There is no limit of Jesus' trust, his hope, his power to endure."

The spiritual classics *The Imitation of Christ* by Thomas à Kempis and *Introduction to the Devout Life* by St Francis de Sales have helped many become more Christ-like as have the contemporary spiritual works of Henri Nouwen, Ruth Burrows, Jacques Philippe, and the Scripture commentaries of the devout Presbyterian William Barclay. To be Christ-like means to eschew all egoism and narcissism and to put Christ and others at the center of our lives so as "to live no longer for ourselves but for him," as one of the Eucharistic prayers says. We are conceived with the *imago Dei* imprinted on our souls; it is our vocation to become *imago Christi* through an ever-greater conformity to the humanity of Christ and his gift to us of his own divine life.

God does not expect something of us that is beyond our human capacity but he does invite us to allow the Holy Spirit to form us into who we are called to be—radiant, unique reflections of Supreme Beauty, God himself. Imagine a stained glass window consisting of several hundred pieces of glass in myriad colors, each one unique. When the light shines through the window, each piece of glass, which was formerly dull and dark, is now illuminated and becomes brilliant and beautiful. The divine life, like the light, takes away nothing of value but it elevates and brings to perfection that which is true, beautiful, and good in every person causing him or her to flourish and shine. In the wondrous diversity of the saints we see how the light of Christ, far from imposing a monotonous uniformity, raises up human masterpieces as dazzlingly different as St John Chrysostom is from St Kateri Tekawitha. Such is the effect of the divine life in us.

By this time you may be asking yourself, "Why haven't I heard about the divine life if it is so important?" Well, you have—under a different name: *grace*.

⇧

A Story from the Desert Fathers
Illustrating the difference between hearing about Jesus
and actually knowing him.

Abba Hilarion said, "Let me tell you a story. Consider the hunting dogs which chase after hares; imagine one of these dogs sees a hare in the distance and immediately gives chase, the other dogs that are with him see this dog taking off and take off after him, even though they have not seen the hare. They will continue running with him, but only for a time; when at length the effort and struggle exhaust them, they give up the chase and turn back. However the dog that saw the hare continues chasing it by himself. He does not allow the effort or the struggle to hinder him from completing his long course. He risks his life as he goes on giving himself no rest. He does not allow the turning aside of the other dogs behind him to put him off. He goes on running until he has caught the hare he saw."[15]

Notes

1   Augustine of Hippo, *Sermo* 117; PL 38, 663 quoted in Thomas Dubay, SM, *God Dwells within Us* (Denville, NJ: Dimension Books, 1971), p. 118.
2   Catherine of Siena, *Dialogue* (trans. Noffke) ch. 37, p. 39.
3   Ps. 42.1
4   C. S. Lewis, *Mere Christianity* (London: Macmillan, 1958), p. 106.
5   John of the Cross, *Spiritual Canticle*, in *The Collected Works of St. John of the Cross* (trans. Kieran Kavanaugh, OCD, and Otilio Rodriguez, OCD; Washington, DC: I.C.S. Publications, 1991), 17:1, p. 542.

6 Vladimir Lossky, *The Mystical Theology of the Eastern Church* (Crestwood, NY: St. Vladimir's Seminary Press, 1976), p. 35.

7 *ST* I, q. 1, a. 9, ad. 3.

8 Prayer 13 in Catherine of Siena, *The Prayers of Catherine of Siena* (ed., trans., notes Suzanne Noffke, OP; San Jose: Authors Choice Press, 2nd edn, 2001), pp. 124–25.

9 Dorothy L. Sayers, *The Greatest Drama Ever Staged* (London: Hodder & Stoughton, 1938), p. 2.

10 *ST* III, q. 3, a. 5.

11 David V. Meconi, SJ, "Deification in the Thought of John Paul II," in *Irish Theological Quarterly* (2006), p. 128.

12 See *ST* III, q. 8, a. 1, ad. 1.

13 Tertullian, *De Res.* 8, 2; PL 2, 852 quoted in CCC, 1015.

14 CCC, 1717.

15 Ernest A. W. Budge (trans.), *The Paradise or Garden of the Holy Fathers* (vol. 2; London: Catto & Windus, 1907), p. 211.

3

Partakers of the divine nature

We have not been made gods from the beginning,
but at first merely men, then at length gods.[1]

ST IRENAEUS OF LYONS

The divine life that God communicates to us in the present life is known as *grace*. The word derives from the Latin *gratia* which is a translation of the Greek word *charis*. In Latin it connotes a favor freely done that affords joy, pleasure, delight, sweetness, charm, and loveliness. But Christianity has long-since "baptized" the word and given it a heightened and more specific meaning. Grace, Aquinas says, "is a participation in the divine nature."[2] The *Catechism* similarly calls grace "a participation in the life of God."[3] We have already said that the soul is the form or spiritual principle of the body. Grace, according to Aquinas, is the accidental form of the soul. The soul is the foundation of our natural existence, but sanctifying grace is the principle of our supernatural, deiform (God-like) life. St Gregory of Nazianzen called grace a "flash of the godhead."[4] One of the loveliest titles of any saint is ascribed to St Dominic: "preacher of grace."

The word *grace* does not appear on the lips of Jesus in the Gospels, but John, in the first chapter of his Gospel, says that "the Word became flesh and lived among . . . full of grace and truth" and the Apostle Paul makes ample use of the word. In 2 Cor. 12.9, for example, he recounts the time the risen Christ told him, "My grace is sufficient for you" in reply to his request that a "thorn" in his side be removed.

Even if Jesus did not use the word, his life manifests the fullness of grace and his parables and teachings illustrate it. The living water which Jesus offers to the Samaritan woman at the well (Jn 4) is interpreted by the Fathers as referring to grace, the divine life, or Christ himself. Likewise, when Jesus urges us to work for "the food that endures for eternal life" (Jn 6.27) the food is seen as symbolic of the same. The garment required for participation in the wedding banquet (Mt. 22.9–14) and the oil in the lamps of the five wise bridesmaids (Mt. 25.1–13) who are awaiting the arrival of the bridegroom have long been interpreted as allusions to grace and its necessity for salvation. The water of life flowing from the throne of God in Rev. 22.1–2 is also regarded as a symbol of the divine life or grace.

Grace is God's action to restore his image in us and to share with us his own divine life. So God-like does grace make us that Irenaeus called it "the seed of the Father," which is perhaps an elaboration on 1 Jn 3.9, "Those who have been born of God do not sin, because God's seed [Greek, *sperma*] abides in them." Grace is the supernatural means to our supernatural end, that is, full communion with the Trinity. It is at the heart of our faith. Perhaps not surprisingly, Catholics and Protestants have differed on the meaning of grace as we will see later.

Channels of grace

The ordinary channel of grace is the Church, the Body of Christ.[5] The sacraments—particularly baptism, penance, and Eucharist— are the "arteries" which convey the divine life to us, not as isolated individuals but as part of the Church or assembly (Greek, *ekklesia*), the convocation of all the baptized—a reality that is both human and divine with Christ as head. Another channel of grace is prayer— and anyone of any faith can pray. Although the normal and most reliable way to grow in grace is as a baptized member of the Body of Christ, we cannot place restrictions on God.

Grace is not a commodity to be procured but a gift to be received. Scripture speaks beautifully of growing in grace.[6] Grace, because it is a participation in God's own life, can never be earned but is always a free gift given to those who truly desire it. Where grace is, Christ is. As we grow in grace, Christ's presence within us also increases. Aquinas says that "grace makes things beautiful."[7]

Grace and nature

One of the most splendidly Catholic of all theological truths was espoused by Aquinas in the opening pages of his *Summa Theologiae*: "grace does not destroy nature but perfects it."[8] In other words, grace and nature (whether human or angelic) are not opposed; each is made for the other. Nature, far from being totally corrupted by sin, is perfectible because it is still fundamentally good having been created by God who continues to sustain its existence or being. Sanctifying grace does not do violence to human nature but elevates it. Grace and human nature go together, and when they come together an amazing new unit is produced: the *deiform* soul.

In classical Protestantism it is said that grace and nature are opposed. The effect of grace on nature, therefore, is to supplant it. The Catholic position regarding human nature, however, reflects the first creation account in Genesis where it is said that "God saw everything that he had made, and indeed, it was very good." It is more optimistic and positive.[9]

Did the first human beings, Adam and Eve, possess sanctifying grace? This question may strike some people as akin to "how many angels can dance on the head of a pin?" and yet the answer—if it can be known—would provide us with an insight into God's original design for man and woman. The consensus of theologians is that Adam and Eve were indeed created in a state of sanctifying grace as suggested by the fellowship they had with God with whom, as Genesis intimates, they would walk "in the garden at the time of the evening breeze."[10]

Grace and graces

Over the centuries, various schools of theology, often identified with the major religious orders such as the Dominicans, Franciscans, and Jesuits, have devised different divisions or classifications of grace. For our purposes I prefer the simple four-fold distinction found in the *Catechism*: sanctifying grace, actual grace, sacramental grace, and special graces, for example, charisms (particular gifts for building up the Body of Christ) and certain states of life such as that of the consecrated religious. The most important grace is *sanctifying grace* which, happily, the *Catechism* refers to as *deifying* grace—because it deifies us or makes us God-like by way of a certain participation.[11] Because over-familiarity with the expression "sanctifying grace" has caused some people not to appreciate the radicalness of its meaning, I prefer to use the expression *deifying grace*. Deifying grace is one of the most exciting and interesting truths of Christianity and has been called the masterpiece of God's handiwork in this world.

Deifying grace is ordinarily first communicated to us at baptism and then increased by the reception of the other sacraments. However, each sacrament also imparts a distinctive *sacramental grace* of its own. For example, the sacramental grace of baptism makes us members of the Church. There are also *actual graces* which are like flares of divine help received for the moment, for a particular action (thus *actual*), or to perform some task. Actual graces which operate on the mind are called *illuminations* and those which operate on the will are *inspirations*. In his loving kindness, God sends actual grace upon actual grace to every human being, whether Christian or not, inviting us to a new way of thinking, loving, and being. For many years I was a missionary in Nigeria and more than once I heard converts to Christianity speak of having experienced earlier in their lives a gentle spiritual "nudge" to enter a Catholic Church when Benediction of the Blessed Sacrament, a most beautiful and unusual ritual, was taking place. Struck by the aesthetics of the ceremony, one thing led to another and eventually the person requested baptism.

Effects of deifying grace

What does deifying grace do? Theologians typically identify four principal effects, all of which ordinarily take place at baptism: justification, the divine indwelling of the Trinity, divine filial adoption, and deification.[12] Let us look briefly at each one.

Justification

Justification is one of those churchy words which we perhaps have heard many times and probably assumed that whatever it means it cannot make much difference in our lives. But it contains some very good news. Justification means to be put right again with God who forgives our sins *and restores us to friendship*. To be "born again" or "born from above" (both are New Testament expressions) is to be justified, according to the Church Fathers. When we were baptized, the stain of sin was washed away. Justification does not make us holy but it places us on the road to God and an increase of deifying grace moves us along it.

Justification is a greater gift than even creation. In creation, we became partakers of the divine *being* or existence but in baptism we are cleansed of all that is contrary to God so that we can be partakers of the divine *life* or nature. The forgiveness that God imparts in justification is not, as Bede Jarrett, OP, points out "a merely negative thing, a removal, a cleansing" but is rather "a return to something great and good and beautiful, the triumphant entrance into the soul of the Father, the Son, and the Spirit."[13] Jarrett then goes on to illustrate the meaning of justification by contrasting it with the traditional Protestant teaching on the subject: "Briefly . . . it may be stated that [the Catholic doctrine of justification] is not simply that God does not impute evil, but He forgives it. It is as though a rebellion had taken place and its leader had been captured and brought before his offended sovereign. Now, the king might do either of two things if he wished not to punish the culprit. He might simply bid him go off and never appear again, or he might go even further by actually forgiving the rebellion and receiving the rebel back into favor. It is one thing to say that no punishment will be awarded; it is another to say that the crime is forgiven, and that everything is to go on as though nothing had happened. In the first case, we might say that the king chose not to impute sin; in the other, that he forgave and justified the sinner. It is just this, then, that the Catholic Church means when She teaches justification as implied in the idea of forgiveness. It is just this, too, that our Lord meant when He detailed His beautiful parable about the prodigal son. The boy's return home does not mean merely that the father refrains from punishment, but rather that there is a welcome so hearty and so complete that the serious-minded elder brother, coming in from his long labor in the fields, is rather scandalized by its suddenness . . ."[14] To have one's sins not only forgiven but forgotten and to be restored to friendship with God as if nothing had happened is indeed good news.

Divine indwelling of the Trinity

The indwelling of the Trinity in the souls of the just is another principal effect of deifying grace. In one sense, it could be said that the whole purpose of Christ's death on the Cross was for the indwelling of the Trinity. Regardless of whether one is baptized or not, God exists everywhere and in everything and sustains everything in being (the doctrine of divine omnipresence or ubiquity). Our being or existence is a participation in God's existence who is Supreme Being. It is in this way that God is present in *every* human person, whether saint or sinner, Christian or not.

The Hebrew people of the Old Testament era had a sense of God's presence insofar as they felt his closeness and concern. They recognized his presence among his Chosen People as well as in the Ark of the Covenant in the Temple and in certain individuals like Abraham and Moses. They looked forward to the time that the prophecy in Zech 2.10 would be perfectly fulfilled: "Sing and rejoice, O daughter Zion! For lo, I will come and dwell in your midst." But the Old Testament was not the era of grace that would be ushered in later by Christ. All the holy men and women of that time were instruments of grace in that God acted on them but not in them as seen, in the opinion of some spiritual writers, in the shining skin of Moses' face after he had spoken with God.[15] With the coming of Christ, however, God now *abides, dwells or lives* in us instead of only sustaining our existence. The New Testament, especially the Johannine literature, abounds with references to the remarkable truth that God actually dwells in us through grace—and because his unlimited presence surrounds us and goes beyond us, we also dwell in him: "On that day you will know that I am in my Father, and you in me, and I in you" (Jn 14.20); "Those who love me will keep my word, and my Father will love them, and we will come to them and make our home with them" (Jn 14.23); "Abide in me as I abide in you. Just as the branch cannot bear fruit by itself unless it abides in the vine, neither can you unless you abide in me"(Jn 15.4); "By this we know that we abide in him and he in us, because he has given us of his Spirit" (1 Jn 4.13); "Do you not know that you are God's temple and that God's Spirit dwells in you?" (1 Cor. 3.16).

It is a mystery that deifying grace, which is created by God, is the channel through which the Divine Indwelling, God himself who is *uncreated grace*, comes to live in the soul. Deifying grace is the necessary disposition for the indwelling Trinity. Theologians have said that there are only three other examples of uncreated grace: the hypostatic union (in which the Second Person of the Trinity unites with human nature), the Beatific Vision, and the real presence of Christ in the Eucharist.

Through the divine indwelling, Christ lives in us and we are, here and now, united to God in this life if we are in a state of grace, that is, free of unrepented grave sin. There is a direct connection between the divine indwelling and the beatific vision in heaven. The former is the seed of the latter. The beatific vision or full communion with the Trinity is a consummation of the extent to which the Trinity dwelt in us at the end of our earthly pilgrimage. The reason the divine indwelling of the Trinity is sometimes referred to as the indwelling of the Holy Spirit is found in Rom. 5.5 where Paul says that "God's love has been poured into our hearts through the Holy Spirit." Another reason is that the work of deification is attributed traditionally to the Holy Spirit.

The divine indwelling is not an invention of medieval theologians because we know that the early Christians were well aware of it. Eusebius, the fourth-century historian of the early Church, relates in his *History* that the father of Origen, the great theologian, used to kneel by the bedside of his sleeping son and reverently kiss his breast as the tabernacle in which God dwells. Early Christians believed that Christ dwelling in the soul revealed himself in a visible way to martyrs at the moment of death. When the Roman martyr Carpus was being burned alive he was asked by a spectator why he was smiling, he replied: "I have seen the glory of the Lord and I am in joy."

The Liturgy of the Eucharist acknowledges in various ways the divine indwelling in those present at Mass. It is because God dwells in the souls of his people that the faithful are incensed by the thurifer; corpses at funerals are also incensed because they once were the temples of the Holy Spirit. When the celebrant says, "The Lord be with you" and the faithful reply, "and with your spirit" they are acknowledging the divine indwelling of the Spirit in the priest. In the *Pax Dei*, the sign of peace, the priest, and the faithful symbolically exchange the indwelling Spirit.

What are the spiritual implications of the divine indwelling for our day-to-day lives? Just as we are influenced by the people who are closest to us, so too does God subtly bring us around to love what he loves and hate what he hates, thereby gradually imparting the divine mind and heart to us. Holiness means responding to the divine presence within us. It is effected from "the inside out" and is therefore unlike other causes which are external to us, such as when a physician gives us an injection to restore our health. Spiritual writers have seen in Jesus' words, "The water that I will give will become in them a spring of water gushing up to eternal life" in the discourse with the woman at the well (Jn 4.14) an allusion to the divine indwelling. The divine indwelling is, in fact, the source of deifying grace in our lives.

Because God dwells in us, we should treasure our bodies and souls—and not only our own, but those of others. As Paul says, "You are not your own" (1 Cor. 6.19). The more we are sensitive to the divine indwelling, the more God will assist us in perceiving Christ in others. The divine presence within us brings about a hunger and thirst for contemplation. Our prayer gradually becomes one with Christ's prayer, and there arises in us a desire to share with others the fruits of one's contemplation.[16] Prayer, in fact, is a response to the divine indwelling.

Sometimes the divine indwelling, which Eastern Christians call the Taboric Light, may result in a mystical experience that imparts an experiential knowledge of God. It is only in heaven, however, that we can have possession of God. Experiences such as so-called "divine touches" may leave us feeling as if we have felt God's presence for the first time. Mystics such as Sts. Catherine of Siena, John of the Cross, and Teresa of Avila, Blessed Henry Suso, and the French Carmelite St Elizabeth of the Trinity (d. 1906) have apprehended the truth of the divine indwelling and have written beautifully about it.[17] Teresa speaks of God as an honored guest in the soul who should not be ignored: "A fine humility it would be if I had the Emperor of Heaven and earth in my house, coming to it to do me a favor and to delight in my company, and I were so humble that I would not answer His questions, nor remain with Him, nor accept what He gave me, but left Him alone. . . . Remember how important it is for you to have understood this truth—that the Lord is within us and that we should be there with Him."[18]

God's presence in us means that we should be prepared for surprises and great changes if we are truly present to him. This is the point C. S. Lewis makes in his classic work *Mere Christianity* where the human person is compared to a house in which God takes up residence: "Imagine yourself as a living house. God comes in to rebuild that house. At first, perhaps, you can understand what He is doing. He is getting the drains right and stopping the leaks in the roof and so on: you knew that those jobs needed doing and so you are not surprised. But presently He starts knocking the house about in a way that hurts abominably and does not seem to make sense. What on earth is He up to? The explanation is that He is building quite a different house from the one you thought of—throwing out a new wing here, putting on an extra floor there, running up towers, making courtyards. You thought you were going to be made into a decent little cottage: but He is building a palace. He intends to come and live in it Himself."[19]

Divine filial adoption

Blessed Columba Marmion, an Irish Benedictine monk and spiritual master who died in 1923, wrote in *Christ in His Mysteries*: "We shall understand nothing—I do not say merely of perfection, but even of simple Christianity—if we do not grasp that its most essential basis is constituted by the state of child of God, participation—through sanctifying grace—in the eternal filiation of the incarnate Word. . . . All Christian life, all holiness, is being by grace what Jesus is by nature: the Son of God."[20]

Divine adoptive filiation constitutes the essence of the Good News. The doctrine appears in the first paragraph of the *Catechism*: "In his Son and through him, God invites men to become in the Holy Spirit, his adopted children and thus heirs of his blessed life." Jesus himself reveals the possibility of a new, filial relationship with the Father when he teaches his disciples to pray: "*Our* Father . . ." Divine filial adoption is alluded to in Paul's letters as well as in the Johannine literature: "But to all who received him, who believed in his name, he gave power to become children of God" (Jn 1.12); "For all who are led by the Spirit of God are children of God. For you did not receive a spirit of slavery to fall back into fear, but you have received a spirit of adoption. When we cry, 'Abba! Father!' it is that very Spirit bearing witness with our spirit that we are children of God, and if children, then heirs, heirs of God and joint heirs with Christ—if, in fact, we suffer with him so that we may also be glorified with him" (Rom. 8.14–17); "He destined us for adoption as his children through Jesus Christ" (Eph. 1.5); "See what love the Father has given us, that we should be called children of God; and that is what we are" (1 Jn 3.1).

To be an adopted child of God may not seem very significant until we consider the great difference between divine and legal adoption. Of course, only Jesus Christ is by nature the Son of God but we are called to become "sons and daughters in the Son" and brothers and sisters of Christ by grace—participation in the divine life. The Spanish Dominican Venerable Juan Gonzalez-Arintero, OP, said that divine filial adoption is not just juridical or some kind of fiction as in the case of legal adoption. In legal adoption, our nature does not change; but in divine filial adoption we are actually infused with the divine life of our heavenly Father. We are not the same. We are transformed into the likeness of Christ and are made co-heirs with him of the Father's wealth. "This heritage," Arintero says, "is not reserved for us for the future only; but He gives it to us immediately and permits us to enjoy even now some of its fruits."[21]

The spirituality of divine filial adoption is the original baptismal devotion of the early Church. It is simply the spirituality of the good son or daughter of God whose exemplar is the Son of God who said of the Father: "I do always the things that please him" (Jn 8.29). Being a son or daughter of God is the fundamental facet of our lives and should determine the way we decide everything. Before the uncertainty of the future and the fragility of human life, the son or daughter of God, like Mary, stands at the foot of the Cross with trusting love and confidence that God is indeed working his purpose out. To be a humble child of God, doing his will, is what Christ meant when he said, "Be perfect, therefore, as your heavenly Father is perfect" (Mt. 5.48). However, being a good son or daughter of God is not instantaneous but continuous and progressive. Sin, on the other hand, is saying to God, "I no longer want to be your son or daughter."

There are several other spiritual truths which derive from divine filial adoption. God loves us not because of anything we do but simply because he has created us and adopted us. He sees and loves in his adopted children what he sees and loves in his Son, to paraphrase one of the prefaces of the Eucharist. Marmion speaks of the "deep interior confidence—composed of liberty of soul and inner joy—of the child who knows he is loved by his Father and, to the best of his weak ability, returns that love."[22] St Josemaría Escrivá (d. 1975) had a strong mystical experience in 1931 which left him profoundly aware of his being an adopted son of God. He wrote: "Divine filiation is a joyful truth, a consoling mystery. It fills all our spiritual life. More than that: precisely because we are children of God, we can contemplate everything in love and wonder as coming from the hands of our Father, God and Creator. And so we become contemplatives in the middle of the world, loving the world."[23]

Filial trust in God our Father is a hallmark of the true son or daughter of God. We should be careful, however, not to project onto God the image and limitations of our own biological fathers but, as Benedict XVI suggests, "let Jesus teach us what *father* really means."[24] Filial, child-like trust is a condition for entering the kingdom of heaven (cf. Mt. 18.3). It allows us to accept what St Catherine once wrote to a correspondent: "You must believe in truth that whatever God gives or permits is for your sanctification."[25] The children of God are marked by a marvelous freedom in which they embrace truth with the sure hope that God can bring to fulfillment all that is good and bring good out of what is not.

Closely related to filial trust is filial obedience. On a day-to-day basis this can take the simple form of responding quickly to the promptings of the Holy Spirit who is constantly working to conform us to the humanity of Christ. In the lives of the saints we often see that there is no time lag between the promptings of the Spirit and their response. Lastly, the prayer of the adopted son or daughter of God is filial and not slavish and fearful. Filial prayer, made with boldness, is prayer characteristic of the New Testament.

On the order of grace, we are brothers and sisters of Jesus Christ and through him brothers and sisters of all the baptized; on the order of nature we are brothers and sisters to all men and women regardless of creed. Jesus died for every man and woman so as "to gather into one the dispersed children of God" (Jn 11.52). In the years since the Second Vatican Council a new emphasis and name has been given to what medieval theologians like Aquinas called legal and distributive justice: social justice. Founded on respect for the human person whose dignity lies in having been created in the image and likeness of God, concern for social justice is further undergirded by the brotherhood and sisterhood of all people. While the Gospel enjoins us to "feed the hungry, give drink to the thirsty, clothe the naked, and give shelter to the homeless," as encapsulated in the six corporal works of mercy, social justice calls us to go beyond individual cases and to examine social systems, laws, and customs which do not contribute to the dignity and full flourishing of any group of people: women, children, the unborn, the poor, immigrants, people of other races, those who think and act differently than us, etc. Working for social justice, according to the *Catechism*, means to "do away with the fears, prejudices, and attitudes of prides and selfishness which obstruct the establishment of truly fraternal societies."[26] This will entail an examination of the root causes of the sinful inequalities that exist in the world. The Second Vatican Council stated: "Excessive economic and social disparity between individuals and peoples of the one human race is a source of scandal and militates against social justice, equity, human dignity, as well as social and international peace."[27] All Christians are called to work for justice which will result in peace, because there can be no lasting peace without genuine justice for all.

Being a good son or daughter of God entails *renunciation* for the sake of the kingdom. "If any want to become my followers, let them deny themselves and take up their cross and follow me" (Mt. 16.24). The supreme example is Jesus before his death when he said: "Father, if you are willing, remove this cup from me; yet, not my will but yours be done" (Lk. 22.42). Renunciation means leaving behind egoism or selfish self-love, but it also means accepting the Cross in one's life. The Cross represents those hard things that God has either willed or allowed to happen and from which he can bring good. We do not choose our crosses—he chooses them for us, and in accepting them in faith and trust instead of defeatist resignation we grow in our relationship with God. As St Catherine wrote: "You must follow him along the way of the cross, choosing to be crucified in his way, not yours."[28] A beautiful insight into the meaning of the Cross is found in a text often ascribed to St. Francis de Sales: "The everlasting God has in His wisdom foreseen from eternity the cross that He now presents to you as a gift from His inmost heart. This cross He now sends you He has considered with His all-knowing eyes, understood with His divine mind, tested with His wise justice,

warmed with loving arms and weighed with His own hands to see
that it be not one inch too large and not one ounce too heavy for
you. He has blessed it with His holy Name, anointed it with His
consolation, taken one last glance at you and your courage, and
then sent it to you from heaven, a special greeting from God to you,
an alms of the all-merciful love of God."[29]

To fight against the selfish desires of the senses through fasting and
other forms of mortification of the flesh has been a part of Christian
life from the beginning. Marie-Dominique Chenu, OP, stated that
"Asceticism should be considered, maintained, and practiced
in the setting of the whole conception of the Christian world."[30]
But asceticism and renunciation are never ends in themselves but
instead are means to breaking the tyranny of the ego. Christianity
is about clearing a way for the infusion of divine life. Catherine
was vehement in her denunciation of any form of asceticism which
did not have as its goal the diminishment of the selfish self-will. An
ancient story from the Desert Fathers illustrates a very simple way
to begin:

> If a traveler is on his way and finds a staff and uses it, he does
> away with much of his journey's labor. So it is in pursuing this way
> of cutting off instinctive desires. From this cutting off of self-will
> a man procures for himself tranquility and from tranquility he
> comes, with the help of God, to serene indifference. In a short
> time a man can cut off ten such desires. He takes a little walk
> and sees something. His thoughts say to him, "Go over there and
> investigate," and he says to his thoughts, "No! I won't," and he cuts
> off his desire. Again he finds someone gossiping, and his thoughts
> say to him, "You go and have a word with them," and he cuts off
> his desire, and does not speak. Or again his thoughts say to him,
> "Go up and ask the cook what's cooking?" and he does not go, but
> cuts off his desire. Then he sees something else and his thoughts say
> to him, "Go down and ask, who brought it?" and he does not ask.
> A man denying himself in this way comes little by little to form a
> habit of it, so that from denying himself in little things, he begins to
> deny himself in great without the least trouble.[31]

For some people, renunciation may also entail a call from God to
go further and freely forego the ownership and use of property,
the enjoyment of marriage, and absolute control over one's life,

all of which, humanly speaking, we are entitled to. Examples of this include the vocation of the consecrated person, that is, nun, monk, friar, virgin, etc., and the celibacy and simplicity of life of the diocesan priest.

One spirituality which derives from the doctrine of divine filial adoption and which countless people have profited from is the "little way" of St Thérèse of Lisieux, a French Carmelite nun who died in 1897 at the age 24. In one of her last conversations before her death she said, "Sanctity does not consist in performing such and such acts; it means being ready at heart to become small and humble in the arms of God, acknowledging our own weaknesses and trusting in His fatherly goodness to the point of audacity."[32]

The French Jesuit Jean Pierre de Caussade (d. 1751) made famous the spirituality of "abandonment to divine providence" or "the sacrament of the present moment" in a collection of letters to nuns published after his death. He encourages us to see in the events of every moment of our lives God's providence and an invitation to grow in holiness. "I believe that people trying to be holy would be saved a lot of trouble if they were taught to follow the right path, and I am writing of people who live ordinary lives in the world and of those specially marked by God. Let the former realize what lies hidden in every moment of the day and the duties each one brings, and let the latter appreciate the fact that things they regard as trivial and of no importance are essential to sanctity. And let them both be aware that holiness means the eager acceptance of every trial sent them by God."[33]

One final consideration: If Jesus is our brother, Mary is then our mother in the order of grace. She was given to us by her Son as one of the final acts of his earthly life: "When Jesus saw his mother and the disciple whom he loved standing beside her, he said to his mother, 'Woman, here is your son.' Then he said to the disciple, 'Here is your mother'" (Jn 19.26–27). From heaven she exercises spiritual motherhood over all her children.

Deification

Deification or divinization is a consequence of divine adoptive filiation. It is the inheritance of the child of God that St Paul refers to in Rom. 8.17. Our inheritance is nothing other than participation in the divine life—the most marvelous gift we could possibly imagine. Deification (Greek, *theosis*) is the most radical and fundamental effect of deifying grace. It is the fulfillment of Christ's words: "I came that they may have life, and have it abundantly." Spiritual writers for centuries have seen allusions to deification in numerous Scripture texts such as the following: "You are gods, children of the Most High, all of you" (Ps. 82.6; see Jn 10.34); "Thus he has given us . . . his precious and very great promises, so that through them you may escape from the corruption that is in the world because of lust, and may become participants of the divine nature"(2 Pet. 1.4); "And all of us, with unveiled faces, seeing the glory of the Lord as though reflected in a mirror, are being transformed into the same image from one degree of glory to another" (2 Cor. 3.18); "For in him the whole fullness of deity dwells bodily, and you have come to fullness in him" (Col. 2.9–10); "Beloved, we are God's children now; what we will be has not yet been revealed. What we do know is this: when he is revealed, we will be like him, for we will see him as he is" (1 Jn 3.2).

The Church Fathers interpreted these texts in striking and almost shocking ways. St Athanasius in the third century said, "God became man so that man might become God."[34] St Cyprian of Carthage, who also lived in the third century, said, "Christ wanted to be what we are so that we could become what Christ is."[35] St Augustine wrote: "God desires to make you a god; not by nature as in his Son, but through grace and adoption."[36]

Deification is also alluded to in numerous prefaces of the Mass and in the prayer the priest says quietly when he puts a drop of water in the wine at the offertory: "By the mystery of this water and wine, may we come to share in the divinity of Christ who humbled himself to share in our humanity." The *Catechism* notes: "Constituted in a state of holiness, man was destined to be fully 'divinized' by God in glory."[37] The implications of deification are made clear by C. S. Lewis: "God said (in the Bible) that we were 'gods' [Ps. 82.6] and He is going to make good His words. If we let Him—for we can prevent Him, if we choose—He will make the feeblest and filthiest of us into a god or goddess, dazzling, radiant, immortal creature, pulsating all through with such energy and joy and wisdom and love as we cannot now imagine, a bright stainless mirror which reflects back to God perfectly (though, of course, on a smaller scale) His boundless power and delight and goodness. The process will be long and in parts very painful; but that is what we are in for."[38]

Deifying grace makes us partakers of God's divine nature and life (they are the same) beginning in this life. Although the process of deification has already begun in baptism we would be wrong to underestimate the difficulty of healing our wounds and putting off the "old man" which cannot be done without violence and pain. "The kingdom of heaven has suffered violence, and the violent"— those willing to engage in spiritual battle—"take it by force" (Mt. 11.12). Mary is the example par excellence of the divinized person who is, as Aquinas is thought to have said, "the place where the Trinity finds its rest" because in her there was no resistance but rather complete receptivity to the Divine.

Deifying grace, because it is created grace, does not actually make us identical to God but it transforms us into an amazing, supernatural likeness to him so that we can truly be called deified. Through grace we participate in a *similitude* or likeness of divine life; only God himself *is* the divine nature and life. God could not possibly give his infinite divine life to finite creatures like ourselves, but he does the next best thing.

Some may wonder if the doctrine of deification is not a repugnant re-appearance of Eve's ill-fated desire to "be like God" when the serpent tempted her (Gen. 3.4) or if it is an errant "new age" belief in Gnostic emanation or pantheistic fusion (*apotheosis*) that has crept into Christianity. The doctrine of deification is entirely different. We are invited by God to *participate* by grace in the divine life of the Son but not to "be" the divine life which Christ is by nature. We are called to be brilliant reflections of Christ who is the "light of the world" (Jn 8.12) and who desires that his disciples be "the light of the world" (Mt. 5.14). The Fathers spoke of the *mysterium lunae*, saying that we are meant to be like the moon which reflects the light of the Sun which is Christ. The moon itself generates no light and can be seen only because it reflects the sun's light. As deifying grace increases in us, the more brilliantly we will reflect the Sun. Regarding Gnosticism and pantheism, Arintero makes it clear that deification "is an ineffable, loving, and free communication, though hidden and inconceivable, of the divine life to rational creatures, wherein the supernatural and the natural, the divine and the human, are conjoined, blended, and intermingled without being fused. God remains ever the same—God is immutable—but man, without ceasing to be man, is deified. Man's integral nature continues, but in another form. Not only is he purified and reinstated in his primitive beauty, but he is raised and elevated to the heights of divinity, brilliantly shining with true divine splendor. He is like the iron which, when placed in the furnace, loses all its dross and, without ceasing to be iron, is turned into fire."[39]

Through the indwelling of the Trinity, each of the divine Persons deifies us from within according to their own properties. The Father imparts his divine being or existence; the Son invites us to grow in his likeness; the Spirit brings us to divine life by pouring charity into our hearts. All three Persons fill us "with all the fullness of God" (Eph. 3.19). The supreme deiform activity will be the Beatific Vision when those who are deified in this life are crowned with full beatitude in the next. Deification, however, is not a solitary process in isolation from others but is attained through Christ and in the Church, the sphere in which union with God takes place in this life.

⇪

Prayer to the Trinity

O consuming Fire! Spirit of love!
Descend within me and reproduce in me, as it were, an incarnation of the Word;
that I may be to him another humanity wherein he renews his mystery.

St Elizabeth of the Trinity

Notes

1 Irenaeus of Lyons, *Against Heresies*, Book 4, ch. 38, no. 4, in *Ante-Nicene Christian Library* (ed. Alexander Roberts, et al; vol. 9; Edinburgh: T&T Clark, 1869), pp. 44–45.
2 *ST* II-II, q. 19, a. 7.
3 CCC, 1997.
4 Gregory Nazianzen, *Dogmatic Poems*, 8; 37, 452, quoted in Olivier Clément, *The Roots of Mysticism. Texts from the Patristic Era with Commentary* (New York: New City, 1995), p. 79.

5   See 1 Cor. 12.12–14
6   See 2 Pet. 3.18.
7   See Thomas Aquinas, *Commentary on the Psalms*, 25, quoted in Anselm Moynihan, OP, *The Presence of God* (Dublin: St. Martin Apostolate, 1948), p. 12.
8   *ST* I, q. 1, a. 8, ad. 2.
9   Gen. 1.31.
10 Gen. 3.8.
11 *CCC*, 1999.
12 See *CCC*, 457–60.
13 Bede Jarrett, OP, *He Dwells in Your Souls* (Manchester, NH: Sophia Institute Press, 1998), p. 46.
14 Ibid., pp. 48–49.
15 See Exod. 34.28–33
16 See *ST* II-II, q. 188, a. 6.
17 See Teresa of Avila, *Way of Perfection*, Book 28; *Life*, 4, 10, 40; John of the Cross, *Spiritual Canticle and Living Flame of Love*; Catherine of Siena, *Dialogue*, ch. 33; Henry Suso, *Little Book of Eternal Wisdom*, p. 15.
18 Teresa of Avila, *Way of Perfection*, Book 28, in Saint Teresa of Avila, *The Complete Works of Saint Teresa of Avila* (trans. E. Allison Peers; vol. 2; London: Sheed & Ward, 1950), pp. 114–15.
19 C. S. Lewis, *Mere Christianity* (London: Macmillan, 1958), p. 160.
20 Blessed Columba Marmion, OSB, *Christ in His Mysteries* (trans. Alan Bancroft; New translation of the original 1924 edition; Bethesda, MD: Zaccheus Press, 2008), pp. 54–55.
21 John G. Arintero, OP, *The Mystical Evolution in the Development and Vitality of the Church* (vol. 1; St. Louis, MO: B. Herder, 1949), p. 87.
22 Columba Marmion, OSB, *Christ the Life of the Soul* (St. Louis, MO: B. Herder, 1925), p. 319.
23 Josemaria Escrivá, *Friends of God: Homilies* (New York: Scepter, 2003), p. 233.
24 Joseph Ratzinger [Pope Benedict XVI], *Jesus of Nazareth: From the Baptism in the Jordan to the Transfiguration* (San Francisco, CA: Ignatius Press, 2008), p. 136.
25 Letter T354 in Catherine of Siena, *The Letters* (trans. Noffke; vol. 4), p. 249.
26 *CCC*, 1931.
27 Second Vatican Council, Pastoral Constitution on the Church in the Modern World *Gaudium et Spes* (December 7, 1965), §29 in *Vatican Council II. The Conciliar and Post Conciliar Documents* (ed. Austin Flannery, OP; vol. 1; 1988 rev. edn; Northport, NY: Costello, 1975), p. 930.

28 Ibid.
29 I have been unable to confirm the authorship of the text.
30 Marie-Dominique Chenu, OP, in *Christian Asceticism and Modern Man* (trans. W. Mitchell and the Carisbrooke Dominicans; New York: Philosophical Library, 1955), p. 163.
31 Dorotheus of Gaza, *Discourses and Sayings* (trans. Eric P. Wheeler; Cistercian Studies Series 33; Kalamazoo: Cistercian Publications, 1977), pp. 88–89.
32 Thérèse of Lisieux, *St. Thérèse of Lisieux. Her Last Conversations* (trans. John Clarke, OCD; Washington, DC: Institute of Carmelite Studies, 1977), p. 129.
33 Jean-Pierre de Caussade, *Abandonment to Divine Providence* (trans. J. Beevers; New York: Image, 1993), ch. I, pp. 8–9, 33–34.
34 Athanasius, *De Incarnatione*, 54, 3; 25, 192b quoted in *CCC*, 460.
35 Cyprian of Carthage, "That Idols are Not Gods," ch. 11, in *Saint Cyprian, Treatises* (trans. and ed. Roy J. Deferrari; The Fathers of the Church. A New Translation; New York: Fathers of the Church, 1958), p. 358.
36 Augustine of Hippo, *Exposition of Psalm 49* in Augustine of Hippo, *Expositions of the Psalms*, pp. 33–50 (trans. Marie Boulding, OSB; The Works of Saint Augustine; A Translation for the 21st Century; Hyde Park: New City Press, 2000), p. 381.
37 *CCC*, 398. For other references to deification in the *Catechism* see 460, 1589, 1988, 1999, 2670.
38 Lewis, *Mere Christianity*, pp. 174–75.
39 John G. Arintero, OP, *The Mystical Evolution in the Development and Vitality of the Church* (trans. Jordan Aumann, OP; vol. 1; St. Louis, MO: B. Herder, 1949), p. 57.

4

A deified mind and heart

*A new heart I will give you, a new spirit I will
put within you. (Ezra 36.26)*

*Let the same mind be in you that was in
Christ Jesus. (Phil. 2.5)*

The process of deification is so profound that it penetrates to the
very core of our substance and elevates our being, faculties, and
actions. Deifying grace makes us a new creation in Christ; it elevates
in a supernatural ("above nature") way our minds and hearts, and
from our deified nature proceed deified actions in our relationships
with others and with God.

When grace is infused into the soul at baptism it brings with it
the *theological virtues* of faith, hope, and charity. They are like the
housewarming gifts that God brings when he dwells in the "house"
of our soul. Deifying grace is not a virtue but rather the foundation
of all infused virtues. The word *virtue* comes from the Latin word
vir which means to be manly, strong, and courageous in the sense
of a fully flourishing human being. The word *virtue* hardly appears
in the pages of the New Testament. However, the concept of divine
powers which God infuses in men and women appears in the letters
of Paul and Peter. Once again, early Christians took a common
word and "baptized" it with a new meaning.

Virtues are stable dispositions that move us toward our final
end, beatitude or full participation in the divine life of the Trinity.
Vices, on the other hand, are stable dispositions that move us in
the opposite direction, away from God and, therefore, away from

our true selves. Some of the vices are pride, selfishness, anger, arrogance, close-mindedness, cowardice, dishonesty, fear, hate, hopelessness, injustice, lust, lying, negative thinking, prejudice, cynicism, resentment, self-condemnation, self-pity, objectification of others, and theft.

Christian tradition distinguishes between *acquired* and *infused* virtues. The principal acquired virtues, which were first identified by the ancient Greeks, are prudence, justice, temperance, and fortitude—the four cardinal virtues. They are called "cardinal" (from the Latin word for *hinge*) virtues because all other human (or moral) virtues—such as humility, kindness, patience, honesty, etc.—are hinged or connected to one or the other. Living a life of prudence, justice, temperance, and fortitude will make for a life of natural happiness. But the definitive supernatural happiness of heaven that we are called to can never be acquired solely by human effort. God "gifts" us with deifying grace and the infused theological virtues of faith, hope, and charity. The acquired virtues, however, can also be elevated by deifying grace and are then infused moral virtues and possess a supernatural quality. All virtues, whether acquired or infused, direct us to God who is Supreme Virtue but only the theological virtues actually reach him. They are called *theological* (God-oriented) for several reasons: because they have God as their proper and immediate object; they are infused by God; and they were revealed by him. The Greeks, who lived before the birth of Christ, were ignorant of faith, hope, and charity as theological virtues.

The theological virtues

It is the Apostle Paul who speaks specifically of the three theological virtues: "And now faith, hope and love abide, these three; and the greatest of these is love" (1 Cor. 13.13); "We always give thanks to God for all of you and mention you in our prayers, constantly remembering before our God and Father your work of faith and labor of love and steadfastness of hope in our Lord Jesus Christ" (1 Thess. 1.3–5); "But since we belong to the day, let us be sober, and put on the breastplate of faith and love, and for a helmet the hope of salvation" (1 Thess. 5.8).

The theological virtues, the *Catechism* says, adapt our intellects and wills "for participation in the divine nature," dispose us "to live in a relationship with the Holy Trinity" and make us "capable of acting as [God's] children and of meriting eternal life."[1] While the world esteems the moral virtues it is not the same with the theological virtues because they draw us away from the natural to the supernatural order.[2]

The theological virtues can lie dormant in the lives of the baptized, as Diadochus of Photke, the fifth-century ascetic and bishop, points out: "When people are baptized, grace hides her presence until the soul makes a decision. When the whole person has turned to the Lord, then with an unspeakable tenderness she reveals her presence to the heart."[3] But God sends actual graces to awaken them and he often does so in the midst of mundane events in which, for example, we are suddenly reminded of God, for example, things that seem coincidental, the chance comment of someone, the kindness of a stranger. "I find just when I need them certain lights that I had not seen until then," St Thérèse of Lisieux wrote, "and it isn't most frequently during my hours of prayer that these are most abundant but rather in the midst of my daily occupations."[4] All moments can be occasions of actual graces. The awakening and increase of faith, hope, and charity is what the Church, the sacraments, the priesthood, and prayer are fundamentally all about.

Jesus Christ the Son of God does not possess the virtues; he *is* Supreme Virtue. To practice the virtues, either by acquiring them or disposing ourselves to receiving them is to participate in the essence of Christ. The virtues are the divine and human characteristics of Christ. With deifying grace, we possess—at least in a germinal way—all of the infused virtues. Education in the virtues in the sense of passing on what the Church teaches about faith, hope, and charity and the cardinal virtues is an important duty of parents, pastors, and teachers. Christ reveals us to ourselves, as the Church teaches in *Gaudium et spes*, and the same can be said of the virtues because they show us who we are called to become as images of Christ.[5]

Let us now look briefly at each of the theological virtues. Keep in mind that, like everything in this book, we are only scratching the surface of an immense body of thought of saints, doctors, popes, mystics, and theologians down through the centuries.

Faith

"Now faith is the assurance of things hoped for, the conviction of things not seen" (Heb. 11.1). Faith is not an intellectual construct but it is, like each of the theological virtues, a gift given by God to those disposed to receive it. Many know about Jesus Christ, but it is only through the gift of faith that we come to know him as Son of God and Savior as well as our brother and friend. Someone could have an advanced degree in theology and still not have received the gift of faith or, having received it, has since rendered it a "dead" faith because of the falsehood of sin. Faith is the theological virtue that elevates the intellect. It is much more than mere belief in the existence of God. The *Catechism* defines faith as "the theological virtue by which we believe in God and believe all that he has said and revealed to us, and that the Holy Church proposes for our belief, because he is truth itself. By faith 'man freely commits his entire self to God.' For this reason the believer seeks to know and do God's will."[6] Faith requires an assent of the intellect and a command of the will but even here God helps us to say Yes. The theological virtue of faith is always united to hope and charity.

Faith transcends reason and yet it is reasonable. Without faith the Good News appears foolish to non-believers. Reason alone can never know the inner life of God, for example, that God is love, that God is not a solitary force of nature but a community of three divine Persons, that he made us in his image and likeness, that he became one of us. God gives us signs to make faith credible. He gives us objective signs like miracles, the fulfillment of prophecies, and the moral miracle of the Church. He also gives us subjective signs like answered prayers, religious experiences, and the Gospel's fulfillment of our spiritual desires. St Catherine says that reason alone gives us a certain amount of knowledge of the truth as we go along our pilgrim way in this life but it is in baptism that we are given a "torch" in which we can see more truth—not all of it, but enough to bring us to our final end. As Paul says, "We walk by faith, not by sight" (2 Cor. 5.7) and in this life "we see in a mirror, dimly" but one day "we will see face to face" (1 Cor. 13.12). In the next life, deifying grace will be crowned with glory and faith will give way to the blessed vision of God, Supreme Beauty, and, to paraphrase one of the most mystical passages of the New

Testament, in seeing him we will be transformed into him.[7] The Jesuit John Hardon describes the difference faith makes in the lives of Christians: "Christians have an evidence of the truth of their religion for which nothing else can supply. They sense that the religion which has power to move them to action is true and to the extent it can renew the human heart it is divine. This is the secret reason why they believe, whether they are adequately conscious of it or not. Their lives are being changed daily in the direction of an unseen power, which only the infused light of God can bring. They have the conviction that a Divine Presence is with them. This Presence becomes stronger according to the length of time they have served God, and as they advance in holiness. They recollect that in the course of years they have become very different from what they once were. They are equally certain that much more than advancing age, outward circumstances, trials and experiences were responsible for the difference."[8]

The contemporary French spiritual writer Jacques Philippe, in his modern spiritual classic *Interior Freedom*, comments on the erodent of faith—doubt: "At the root of sin lies *doubt*, suspicion of God. Is God really as good as he says? Can one trust his word? Is he really Father? Doubt gives rise to *distrust*: we don't believe God can fulfill us and make us happy. Then we try to manage on our own, in disobedience. This is the birth of selfishness, covetousness, lust, jealousy, fear, conflict, violence, and the whole network of evil."[9] But to doubt that God can make us happy is unreasonable and unfair, as the eternal Father once told Catherine:

Why do you not have confidence in me, your Creator? Why do you trust in yourself? Do you not know that I am faithful and loyal to you? [. . .] Redeemed and restored to grace by means of the blood of my only-begotten Son, you have experienced this. But it seems that they do not believe that I am powerful enough to provide for them and strong enough to help them and defend them from their enemies, and wise enough to illuminate the eye of their intellect, or that I have enough clemency to give them what is necessary for salvation. It seems that I am not rich enough to enrich them, not sufficiently beautiful to make them beautiful, that I do not have enough food for them to eat nor clothing for them to wear.[10]

Hope

Hope is perhaps the most ignored and misunderstood of the three theological virtues. It is the divine gift of *trust* that no matter what happens, God lies ahead. Herbert McCabe, OP, the brilliant English theologian, defines hope as: "Confidence that God plans to bring humanity to the Kingdom in Christ and that only unrepented grave sin can exclude us from it."[11] Faith tells us that God desires to share his divine life with us and hope assures us that this is really possible. God is utterly reliable. The glossary of the *Catechism* says that hope is the "theological virtue by which we desire and *expect* from God both eternal life and the grace we need to attain it." Hope elevates the intellect.

The theological virtue of hope is not the same as human optimism. Optimism refers to a positive outlook on life based on favorable signs. It can also refer to what we think we can accomplish or bring about through our own efforts or by chance. There are two vices opposed to hope: *presumption*, which does not take seriously the fact that the object of hope is difficult to obtain, and *despair* which does not take seriously the fact that the object of hope is possible. In heaven, hope will give way to joyful possession of the object of our hope, God himself.

Many people without realizing it trust only in themselves. If they believe in God at all, they may think that they can manipulate him through prayers and actions. Often, however, we can fully receive this beautiful virtue only when we have experienced our own misery and poverty apart from God. "God waits for our tears," St Ambrose said, "that he may pour forth his goodness." When our hearts have been ploughed by a crisis we may then realize for the first time how powerless we actually are and how pointless it is to trust in ourselves and we are now disposed to receive God's gift of hope or trust in him. Hope is the trust that allows one to lay his or her head on the breast of Christ, as the apostle John did at the Last Supper, and leave it there. Aquinas says that Christian hope is "clinging to God."[12] We trust Christ to reach out and save us in the midst of the storm. Hope lovingly invites us to lay down our innate egoism, that is, the desire to control and possess everything, and to serenely surrender to God's will. One indication that we have the virtue of hope is if we pray because it shows that to some extent we have trust in God for our future. Catherine of Siena says that we trust and believe in what we love.[13] The question is: What do we truly love most?

There are many stories of holy people who had the virtue of hope to an heroic degree. In our own time, we have the example of Walter Ciszek (1904–84), an American Jesuit who spent 23 years in prison camps in the Soviet Union. Fr Ciszek describes one of the darkest moments of his imprisonment and the vital presence of hope that he encountered during this time:

> Across the threshold I had been afraid to cross, things suddenly seemed so very simple. There was but a single vision, God, who was all in all; there was but one will that directed all things, God's will. I had only to see it, to discern it in every circumstance in which I found myself, and let myself be ruled by it. God is in all things, sustains all things, directs all things. To discern this in every situation and circumstance, to see His will in all things, was to accept each circumstance and situation and let oneself be borne along in perfect confidence and trust. Nothing could separate me from Him, because He was in all things. No danger could threaten me, no fear could shake me, except the fear of losing sight of Him. The future, hidden as it was, was hidden in His will and therefore acceptable to me no matter what it might bring. The past, with all its failures, was not forgotten; it remained to remind me of the weakness of human nature and the folly of putting any faith in self. But it no longer depressed me. I looked no longer to self to guide me, relied on it no longer in any way, so it could not again fail me. By renouncing, finally and completely, all control of my life and future destiny, I was relieved as a consequence of all responsibility. I was freed thereby from anxiety and worry, from every tension, and could float serenely upon the tide of God's sustaining providence in perfect peace of soul.[14]

Charity

Theologians have sometimes distinguished between *charity* and *love*. Love traditionally refers to natural human love, the highest form of which is friendship. Charity, on the other hand, refers to a participation in the divine love that God has for himself and for us. "For me to love You as You love me," said St Thérèse of Lisieux,

"I would have to borrow Your own Love."[15] With the infused theological virtue of charity, we love our neighbor not for our own sake but for God. This is the supernatural love that is charity. Charity elevates the will.

"*Just as I have loved you*, you also should love one another" (Jn 13.34). We should strive to love others, ourselves, and even God with God's own self-sacrificing love and not with just any kind of human love—even the best. The glossary of the *Catechism* defines charity as the "theological virtue by which we love God above all things for his own sake, and our neighbor as ourselves for the love of God." The words "for his own sake" are important because we can deceive ourselves by having mercenary love for God, which we will say more about in Chapter 7. Note that genuine charity includes self-love but not selfish self-love.

The highest of all virtues is charity and sins against it are the greatest. Christian holiness consists primarily in charity. Saints are canonized not because of their intelligence or hard work but because of their charity. Christ, the image of God, is the ultimate object of our charity. Charity is the only theological virtue that we take with us in heaven. The principal vices which are opposed to it are hatred, envy, and jealousy.

Mystics like Catherine of Siena often illumine particular aspects of the faith in ways that are more affective than intellectual. Because charity and love are essential for human life, Catherine hears the eternal Father say to her, "The soul cannot live without love. She always wants to love something because love is the stuff she is made of, and through love I created her."[16] She repeatedly reminds us that love follows knowledge.[17] "One who knows more, loves more."[18] We love God the more we come to know his love for us and so Catherine constantly enjoins us to "open the eye of the intellect" and to gaze at the Crucified One. With a practical knowledge of human psychology, she warns us against a false love of God which would isolate us from loving others: "Love for our creator cannot be sustained unless we love others for God's sake."[19]

The acclaimed Orthodox theologian Olivier Clément, in his survey of Eastern Christian mysticism, notes that for anyone who wants to grow in holiness, "nothing is more important than the Gospel command, 'Do not judge.'"[20] Catherine insisted that we must not judge others. "She ruled out of her life," Raymond of

Capua says in his biography of her, "any passing of judgment on her neighbor, be it lawful or unlawful, and renounced all concern about how people might judge herself."[21]

The Gifts of the Holy Spirit

The theological virtues are exercised according to a human mode in that they follow the dictates of reason illumined by faith. Aquinas, however, says that the infused virtues, both moral and theological, if they are to be truly proportioned to the supernatural life of communion with the Trinity, must be perfected by the Gifts of the Holy Spirit. This is because the infused virtues are guided by reason which alone cannot reach God. According to Aquinas, the Gifts are necessary for salvation because they prepare us for the beatific vision.[22] The Gifts are not external to the infused virtues but derive from them; they perfect the infused virtues from within.

Although the *seven* Gifts of the Holy Spirit are not explicitly mentioned in Scripture, St Paul speaks of gifts of the Holy Spirit without enumerating them.[23] The origin of the number seven is Isa. 11.2 where six spiritual characteristics of the future Messiah-King are mentioned: wisdom, understanding, counsel, might (fortitude), knowledge, and fear of the Lord. The Septuagint (Greek Old Testament) added *piety* to make seven, the biblical number of plenitude. The *Catechism* retains the tradition of the seven Gifts and names them.[24]

All the Gifts are bestowed in baptism and strengthened in the sacrament of confirmation. The general effect of the Gifts is to perfect the infused virtues by making them flexible, docile, and sensitive to the promptings of the Holy Spirit. Since our final end is communion with the Trinity, our actions must be proportioned not just to human nature but to divine nature. As a scholastic axiom says, "All means must be proportional to their ends." The Gifts impart a divine mode to our human actions. The Portugese Dominican John of St Thomas (d. 1644) compared the soul to a boat which at first is carried forward by rowing, representing the infused virtues in which we retain the direction of our actions by the use of our reason. But when a sail, representing the Gifts of the Holy Spirit, is hoisted, the boat catches the inspirations of the Spirit and sails along with greater constancy and in the direction that the Spirit blows, taking it at times to destinations never imagined.[25]

Growth in holiness is essentially a matter of responding quickly and generously every time to the promptings of the Holy Spirit. In each moment of the day, God invites us to a closer relationship with him. Good times are occasions for expressions of thanksgiving and praise; difficult times for expressions of faith and trust in God; temptations and memories of our past life can be occasions for sorrow; the needs of others are invitations to intercessory prayer.

The Gifts can be seen in the marvelous spontaneity of the saints who were no longer guided by slow human reason (which will often take into consideration the many reasons for *not* acting) but who perceived clearly God's will and did it immediately no matter how imprudent it may have seemed to others. The Gifts cause us to march to the beat of a different Drummer, one who is no longer only human but also divine. It is for this reason that the actions of the saints may sometime seem absurd. A year after founding the Order of Preachers in 1216, St Dominic boldly sent seven of his sixteen friars to Paris—an action which seemed nearly suicidal for the fledgling group but which he defended by saying, "Hoarded grain rots." One of the most extreme examples of divine absurdity is St Benedict Joseph Labré (d. 1783), a French layman who lived outdoors in the Coliseum in Rome for many years. History abounds in stories of saints who immediately gave whatever food or clothing they had to someone in need. The spontaneous decision of martyrs not to betray their faith and to accept death is another example.

Besides making the theological virtues sensitive and docile to the promptings of the Holy Spirit, the Gifts infuse *affective* knowledge of God in that they allow us to experience our relationship with him in ways that pertain to feeling, touching, and tasting. Now our knowledge of God is not so much intellectual as it is intuitive and instinctive.

Using Aristotelian categories, Aquinas proposed an elaborate schema in which he shows how an individual Gift corresponds to one or more of the seven infused theological and cardinal virtues as well as to each of the Beatitudes. For our purposes, we will briefly examine only the four Gifts which, according to him, perfect the theological virtues of faith, hope, and charity.

The Gifts of Understanding and Knowledge

These two Gifts perfect the theological virtue of faith, but each does so in a different way.

The *Gift of Understanding* is the gift of insightful faith. It imparts a deeper apprehension or intuition of the meaning of familiar religious images, words, and faith statements. It helps us to understand more deeply some article of faith and to see how it applies to our daily lives. Furthermore, it gives us a sense of when something pertaining to faith and morals is not being interpreted correctly.[26] St Augustine of Hippo's profound penetration and assimilation of the truths of the faith exemplify this Gift as seen, to give just one example, in his well-known statement: "*Noverim te, noverim me*"—May I know You so that I may know myself.[27]

The *Gift of Knowledge* is the gift of mature faith. Aquinas says that this Gift is one of judgment. While the aforementioned Gift of Understanding helps us to penetrate to the core meaning of our faith, the Gift of Knowledge helps us to judge wisely as to the theoretical and practical consequences of an insightful faith. This Gift helps us to integrate our secular knowledge with our faith, which is sorely needed today. St Athanasius, the third-century bishop of Alexandria and tireless defender of the divinity and humanity of Christ who was ousted from his episcopal see at least five times because of his orthodoxy, exemplifies this Gift. He realized the implications if Jesus was only the Son of Man and not the Son of God when he defended the divinity of Christ in his work *On the Incarnation*. "Dead men cannot take effective action; their power of influence on others lasts only till the grave. Deeds and actions that energize others belong only to the living. Well, then, look at the facts in this case. The Savior is working mightily among men, every day He is invisibly persuading numbers of people all over the world, both within and beyond the Greek-speaking world, to accept His faith and be obedient to His teaching. Can anyone, in face of this, still doubt that He has risen and lives, or rather that He is Himself the Life? Does a dead man prick the consciences of men . . .?"[28]

The Gift of Fear of the Lord

This is the Gift of *reverence* which perfects the theological virtue of hope. It does not make us afraid of God but rather fills us with wonder and awe before him. It helps us see that God is infinitely more powerful than ourselves and so it inclines us not to trust in ourselves or in anything for our salvation but to place all our trust in him alone. In this way the Gift of reverence facilitates the virtue of hope.

St Paul exemplifies this Gift as seen in the account of his conversion in Acts 9. Thrown to the ground and blinded, the Apostle was helpless when he heard the voice of the Lord. Trusting in him, Paul allowed himself to be led by the hand to Damascus where his conversion was completed.

The Gift of Wisdom

It may seem odd that the Gift of Wisdom is the one that perfects charity, the most important theological virtue. In ordinary parlance the word *wisdom* means accumulated knowledge and erudition. But the wisdom that is a Gift of the Holy Spirit takes it meaning from the Latin word for wisdom, *sapientia*, the root meaning of which is "to taste." In the lives of the great mystics there is a point when they came to "taste" God for the first time, that is, to have an affective encounter with him. This is the result of the unfolding of baptismal grace. We can see evidence of the Gift of Wisdom in Catherine of Siena's great hymn of praise in the last chapter of her *Dialogue* when she exalts: "For by the light of understanding within your light, I have *tasted* and seen your depth, eternal Trinity, and the beauty of your creation."[29]

It is the Gift of Wisdom that imparts love-knowledge of the Lord, the knowledge a lover has of the beloved. It is also the gift that helps us to love others the way God loves them. The Immaculate Virgin Mary, whose mind and heart were fully deified, exemplifies the Gift of Wisdom because hers was pre-eminently a love-knowledge of Jesus, Son of God, and her own son. This is why John Paul II more than once encouraged the faithful to contemplate the face of Jesus through the eyes of the one who loved him most, his mother Mary.[30]

Regarding the infused cardinal virtues, Aquinas says that the *Gift of Counsel* or decision-making perfects prudence; the *Gift of Piety* or being a good son or daughter of God perfects justice; the *Gift of Fortitude* or courage perfects fortitude; and the *Gift of Fear of God* or reverence perfects temperance.

It is important to note that "grace escapes our feelings," as the *Catechism* says.[31] Feelings are not always reliable indicators of whether Christ lives in us, that is, that we are in a state of grace. Gladness, Catherine points out, only means that we have gotten what we wanted.[32] This predicament of not knowing underscores the importance of frequent participation in the sacrament of confession (penance, reconciliation) as well as the importance of a spiritual director. One traditional practice in this regard is the daily examination of conscience often referred to as the *examen*. However, Christ did say, "You will know them by their fruits" (Mt. 7.16). The fruits of the Holy Spirit (charity, joy, peace, patience, kindness, goodness, generosity, gentleness, faithfulness, modesty, self-control, chastity) enumerated in Gal. 5.22–23 of the Vulgate Bible are regarded as the first fruits of eternal glory. In a similar way, the Beatitudes (Mt. 5.3–12; Lk. 6.20–22) "shed light on the actions and attitudes characteristic of the Christian life."[33]

The Fathers of the Church emphasized the importance of the virtues as something positive that we should aspire to. Nonetheless, obeying God's will as found in the Ten Commandments is absolutely essential to being open to God's gifts of faith, hope, and charity. The Commandments clear the ground for God to begin building his spiritual edifice in our souls.

⇑

The great Christian mystics had the Gifts of Wisdom, Knowledge and Understanding to a high degree. Catherine of Siena gives us a marvelous glimpse into the world of a saint whose intellect and will had been deified by the infused virtues and Gifts of the Holy Spirit. She once shared with Raymond of Capua, her confessor and friend, the atmosphere in which a deified soul lives. It is, she said, as if the soul plunges into a divine sea and thereafter sees everyone and everything through the medium of divine omnipresence. Here is Raymond's account of what Catherine told him: "The soul which sees that it itself is nothing, and which knows that all its good is in its Creator, turns its back, with all the powers of its being, on itself and every creature, and plunges itself totally in its Creator. From [then] on it directs all it does, above all and throughout all, to him. Its whole mind is set on never going one step outside of him in whom it realizes it has found its whole good and its complete and perfect happiness. This union of love grows daily more intense, and eventually the soul is, in a manner, so transformed into God that all its thoughts—its understanding and its love and its memory—are taken up exclusively with God, and busy about God alone. Itself and other creatures it sees only in God; it thinks of them and of itself exclusively in God. It is like what happens when a person dives into the sea and swims underwater. He sees nothing and touches nothing but the water and whatever is submerged in the water. Outside the water he sees nothing, feels nothing, and touches nothing. And if the images of the things outside fall in or on the water, he does not see them as they are in themselves, but only as they are or appear in the water. To envisage things in this way means that love of self and of other creatures is now brought under the rule of right order, and can no longer stray beyond its proper bounds. It is now subjected to a rule which is divine. Existing and acting only in God, it no longer lusts after anything outside of God."[34]

Notes

1   CCC, 1812–13.
2   See Jordan Aumann, OP, *Spiritual Theology* (London: Sheed & Ward, 1980), p. 248.
3   Diadochus of Photke, *Gnostic Chapters*, 85; *Sources Chretiénnes 5 bis*, p. 144 quoted in Clément, *The Roots of Christian Mysticism*, p. 190.
4   Thérèse of Lisieux, *Story of a Soul. The Autobiography of St. Thérèse of Lisieux* (trans. by John Clarke, OCD; Washington, DC: Institute of Carmelite Studies, 3rd edn, 1996), p. 179.
5   *Gaudium et Spes*, §22, 922.
6   CCC, 1814.
7   See 1 Jn 3.2–3.
8   John Hardon, SJ, *History and Theology of Grace* (Ann Arbor, MI: Veritas Press, 2003), pp. 340–41.
9   Jacques Philippe, *Interior Freedom* (New York: Scepter Press, 2007), p. 108.
10 S. Caterina da Siena, *Il Dialogo*, ch. CXL, a cura di G. Cavallini (Roma: Edizioni Cateriniane, 1968), pp. 385–86. My translation.
11 Herbert McCabe, OP, *Teaching of the Catholic Church* (London: Darton, Longmann & Todd, 2000), p. 82.

12 *ST* II-II, q. 17, a. 6.
13 See Catherine of Siena, *Dialogue* (trans. Noffke), ch. 8, p. 38.
14 Walter Ciszek, SJ, *He Leadeth Me* (Garden City: Doubleday, 1973), p. 79.
15 Thérèse of Lisieux, *Story of a Soul*, p. 256
16 Catherine of Siena, *Dialogue* (trans. Noffke), ch. 51, p. 103.
17 See ibid., ch. 1, p. 25.
18 Ibid., ch. 66, p. 126.
19 Letter T343 in Catherine of Siena, *The Letters* (trans. Noffke; vol. 4), p. 267.
20 Clément, *The Roots of Christian Mysticism*, p. 281.
21 Raymond of Capua, *The Life of Catherine of Siena* (trans. Conleth Kearns, OP; Wilmington, DE: Michael Glazier, 1980), §370, p. 343. For more on passing judgment, see Catherine of Siena, *Dialogue* (trans. Noffke), ch. 108, p. 202.
22 *ST* I-II, q. 68, a. 2.
23 See 1 Cor. 12.4.
24 CCC, 1831.
25 "With only the virtues, even though they are supernatural, man is like an apprentice who knows fairly well what he must do, but who has not the skill to do it in a suitable manner. Consequently, the master must come from time to time, take his hand, and direct it so that the work may be presentable." Reginald Garrigou-Lagrange, OP, *Christian Perfection and Contemplation* (St Louis, MO: B. Herder, 1937), p. 282.
26 See Benedict Ashley, OP, *Living the Truth in Love. A Biblical Introduction to Moral Theology* (Staten Island, NY: Alba House, 1996). See also his "Gifts of the Holy Spirit" at www.domcentral.org.
27 See Augustine of Hippo, *Soliloquies*, Book 2, 1 in Saint Augustine, *Soliloquies. Augustine's Interior Dialogue* (trans. and notes by Kim Paffenroth; The Augustine Series; Hyde Park: New City Press, 2000), p. 55.
28 Athanaisus, *St. Athanasius on the Incarnation*, 30, (intro. C. S. Lewis; trans. and ed. religious of the CSMV; Crestwood, NY: St. Vladimir's Seminary Press, 1993), p. 60.
29 Catherine of Siena, *Dialogue* (trans. Noffke) ch. 167, p. 365.
30 Pope John Paul II, Apostolic Letter *Rosarium Virginis Mariae* (October 16, 2002), §1, at the Holy See, www.vatican.va.
31 CCC, 2005.
32 Catherine of Siena, *Dialogue* (trans. Noffke), ch. 106, p. 199.
33 CCC, 1717.
34 Raymond of Capua, *The Life of Catherine of Siena* (trans. Kearns), §100, pp. 92–93.

5

The reign of God

*The Church will appear in its eternal glory
as the Kingdom of God.
It is the sphere within which union with God
takes place in this present life.*[1]

VLADIMIR LOSSKY

Pope Benedict XVI, in the first volume of his trilogy *Jesus of Nazareth*, says that "the core of the Gospel is this: *The Kingdom of God is at hand.*"[2] This should not come as a surprise since Jesus frequently spoke of the kingdom of God (or of heaven) as near and sent his disciples out to proclaim it. He also taught them to pray "Your kingdom come" in the Lord's Prayer. Yet, how many people have a clear idea of what Jesus meant? Perhaps many think that the expression simply refers to the afterlife or the second coming of Christ.

The Greek word *basileia*, which originally referred to a royal palace, can be translated as kingship, kingdom, or reign. Scripture scholars agree that the New Testament expression *kingdom of God* indicates the rule, kingship, or *reign* of God. The word "reign" instead of the more familiar "kingdom" conveys better in English the act of holding sway in the hearts of men and women. In the writings of the Church Fathers, as Benedict XVI observes, the expression has three different meanings. The first one, which comes from Origen, is that Jesus himself is the kingdom in person. The second, also from Origen, "sees man's interiority as the essential location of the kingdom." The third dimension, he says, "we could call the ecclesiastical: the Kingdom of God and the Church are related in different ways and brought into more or less close proximity."[3]

The kingdom has indeed come in the person of Christ who inaugurates it on earth as the Church but it is also within us because of his abiding presence in the soul.[4] The kingdom is the realm of the divine presence. Jesus' invitation to enter the kingdom comes in the form of parables in which we are called to enter a new field of energy through repentance and conversion (Greek, *metanoia*). As the English Salvatorian Bernard Green notes:

> It is to the call of the Spirit, operating in the depths of our being and calling us to the realization of the image of Christ within us in our own unique way that the *metanoic* process of transformation is related. It is to the on-going realization of ever-increasing unity and integrity within our being and the consequent realization of higher human potential. The call to repentance and conversion, therefore, far from having the quality of being a somber and fearful thing is something one can embrace with enthusiasm. The parables of Jesus portray the process as something a person will give himself over to whole-heartedly, it is something one wants to do in order to attain the joy and peace of a higher level of being. One has been able to glimpse the value of this higher form of living and will pay any price to lay hold of it completely. The kingdom is that "pearl of great price", that "coin" one will search endlessly for, the treasure in the field. Nothing will prevent one from seeking to enter into it, not one's foot, or eye or any other aspect of one's reality. All are of lesser importance,—and are experienced as such,—than the experience of being in the kingdom.[5]

After an extensive ministry of healing and teaching in which he frequently announced that the kingdom was present, Jesus' final words to his followers in Mt. 28.19 are seemingly devoid of any reference to it when he commands them to "Go therefore and make disciples of all nations, baptizing them in the name of the Father and of the Son and of the Holy Spirit." Baptism, of course, is the rite of incorporation into the Church. What is the relation between the kingdom and the Church? The Second Vatican Council said that the Church "is the kingdom of Christ already present in mystery" and that she is "on earth the seed and the beginning of that kingdom."[6]

The Church, the Body of Christ

The more deified we are the less we are separated from others. The more we love God, the more we love what he loves—ourselves and other people. Increasing union with God is mirrored in increasing presence to our neighbor, as the sixth-century monk Dorotheus of Gaza says: "This is the nature of love: to the extent that we distance ourselves from the center [of the circle] and do not love God, we distance ourselves from our neighbor; but if we love God, then the nearer we draw to him in love, the more we are united with our neighbor in love."[7]

Because it is the Body of Christ (1 Cor. 12.12–14), the Church mediates the presence of the Spirit of Christ. It is the means of communion with God and with one another in Christ. The Church Fathers saw in the flow of blood and water from the side of the crucified Christ the emergence of the Church, the new Eve just as the first Eve had come from Adam's side. Many people, however, have an impoverished idea of the Church and see it merely as a human institution that is fallible and sinful. The Church is not only human but also divine. St Paul calls the Church the Body of Christ and the Spouse of Christ (Eph. 5.22–33), the two images of the Church among others which most relate to spiritual growth. The institution, as Olivier Clément observes, "is merely the visible aspect of the 'mystery.'"[8] Writing in 1928, the Venerable Juan González Arintero, OP, made this bold but true statement: "Without an exposition, however brief, of the basis of the spiritual life and the growth in Christian perfection, the defense of our religion would always be incomplete and defective. To make God's Church loved, no better way can be found than to show the ineffable attractions of its inner life. To present only its inflexible exterior aspect is almost to disfigure it and make it disagreeable; it is, in a sense, to despoil it of its glory and its principal enchantments. All its glory is from within."[9]

Indeed deep within the mystery of the Church there is a great liberality and gentleness that often goes unrecognized. The Second Vatican Council, for example, affirmed the Church's ancient belief that those who do not know Christ can be saved: "Those who, through no fault of their own, do not know the Gospel of Christ or his Church, but who nevertheless seek God with a sincere heart, and, moved by grace, try in their own actions to do this will as they know it through the dictates of their conscience—those too may achieve salvation."[10] Perhaps for many Catholics the most common experience of the Church's understanding and gentleness is in the confessional. T. S. Eliot once said that the Church was "tender when men would be hard, and hard when they would like to be soft."[11]

In the lives of the saints and mystics we see how their love for Jesus expands and is transformed into love for his Body the Church. Jacques Philippe notes that "contemplation brings us into the heart of the mystery of the Church. . . . The grace of prayer always integrates the one praying more fully into the mystery of the Church."[12] There is no genuine or life-giving spirituality which is outside or above it. St Teresa of Avila, like her contemporary St John of the Cross, suffered greatly during her lifetime because of the misunderstanding and suspicion of Church authorities and co-religious. Despite this, Teresa's dying words were, "*I am a daughter of the Church.*"

Membership in the Church is not an abstraction as it entails our actual insertion in a local community with all its faults as well as its ability to mirror back to us, providing we are open and truly desire to know ourselves, the actual quality of our faith, hope, and charity. Our pilgrimage to God is always communitarian in the context of the Church, the parish or, for consecrated persons, the religious community. As human beings, we have a great capacity for being blind to who and what we really are, but participation in parish life can challenge our self-perceptions and be a channel for God's invitation for us to come closer. No one has spoken more strongly on the importance of involvement in the Christian community than the Canadian Oblate of Mary Immaculate Ronald Rolheiser: "In community the truth emerges and fantasies are dispelled. Not being involved with church because of the church's faults is often a great rationalization. What is too painful to deal with is not the church's imperfection but my own fantasies about my own goodness, which, in the grind of real community, will become painfully obvious. Nobody deflates us more than does our own family. The same is true of the church. Not all of this is bad."[13]

The sacraments

Using Paul's image of the Church as the Body of Christ, it could also be said that the Holy Spirit is its heart and the sacraments are the arteries through which the blood of divine life flows. Prayer, which we will consider in the next chapter, is also a channel of deifying grace. Of the seven sacraments, the most indispensable are baptism and the Eucharist. Aquinas says that the sacraments apply the effects of Christ's passion to us.[14] The instrument of the divine life, as we have said, is the humanity of Christ. The flow of blood and water from Christ's pierced side has also been seen for centuries as a symbol of baptism and the Eucharist.

Aquinas notes that "Baptism is the beginning of the spiritual life, and the door of the sacraments; whereas the Eucharist is, as it were, the consummation of the spiritual life, and the end of all the sacraments."[15] Baptism imprints a seal or character on the soul, as a signet ring in ancient times made an impression on sealing wax. This seal orients us to the likeness of Christ and perfects the *imago Dei* by the Spirit re-creating us as *imago Christi*.

The Holy Spirit, seen as the life-giving breath of the risen Christ in Jn 20.22, is conferred on us in a particular way in the sacraments. *Baptism* signifies new birth; the *Eucharist* is the sacrament of union; *Confirmation* completes the grace of Baptism by an increased outpouring of the Gifts of the Holy Spirit; *Penance* signifies resurrection; *Anointing of the Sick* soothes and comforts against spiritual sorrows and weaknesses; *Matrimony* confers on husband and wife the graces necessary for a holy and faithful union which mirrors the union of Christ and his Bride the Church; the sacrament of *Holy Orders* consecrates men as dispensers of Christ's sacred mysteries and distributors of his graces. As noted in Chapter 3, each sacrament confers deifying grace as well as its own particular sacramental grace.

Worship and liturgy

[Priest:] *Let us give thanks to the Lord our God.*
[People:] *It is right and just.*

Roman Missal

Worship is an acquired moral virtue which is related to the cardinal virtue of justice. The notion of worship as rendering to God something due to him who is the source of all being is largely forgotten today in our culture where entertainment, affirmation, and promises of rewards are the preferred forms of "worship." But human beings, it should be noted, attain self-fulfillment in giving themselves to others and, in a supreme way, to God. As Green points out:

> Human beings, if they are to be human, to retain their humanity and develop their humanness, must worship God and learn to reject all idols in order to discern the face of God, a face that is not its own. To 'be' fully, the Being of God must be chosen as central, not the being of self. The narcissistic 'self', that sees itself as the most important of beings, the one around which the world should revolve, must ever die that the higher 'self' may always be emerging. It dies in true worship. Worship is essential to us becoming humble, truly ourselves.[16]

Only when we are detached from selfish self-love and other forms of self-preoccupation are we truly free to praise and adore God. We flourish as human beings when we have grateful hearts. We should strive to let the words of this simple prayer become our own: "*Lord, take me from myself and give me to yourself.*"

The twofold goal of the liturgy, the Church's official public worship (the celebration of the sacraments and the Liturgy of the Hours), is the glorification of God and the deification of the faithful.

The Eucharist: Source and summit of Christian life

Ever since Christ said to his disciples at the Last Supper, "Do this in memory of me," Christians have worshipped God by celebrating the sacrament of the Lord's Supper known as the Eucharist, the Mass, or the Divine Liturgy. St Paul alludes to the Eucharist in 1 Cor. 11.17–34; the writer of the late first-century or early second-century document known as the *Didache* describes in a general way the same Eucharistic ritual as the one that took place in Corinth; the ancient work *Apostolic Tradition* attributed to Hippolytus of Rome, which has been dated as early as AD 215, gives a more detailed account of how the same Eucharist was celebrated.

The Eucharist is the chief sacrament because, unlike the other sacraments, it does not just apply the power of Christ but *contains Christ himself* so that the Eucharist is indeed the "source and summit of the whole Christian life."[17] It contains not only grace but the Author of grace; all the other sacraments are directed toward it. "It is the sacrament of union," says Aquinas. "Its first effect is to unite, not that it produces the first union, but it fortifies that which is already contracted."[18]

In the Old Testament the sacrifice of animals was a sign or prefiguration of the future definitive sacrifice of Christ on the Cross. The sacraments of the New Testament, however, are much more than mere signs because, unlike the Old Testament sacrifices, they are channels of grace. From the earliest times the Church has believed that Christ is really present in the Eucharist as he is in heaven, but in a different way. In heaven Christ is present in his natural presence as he appears, but on earth his real presence is his sacramental presence, that is, under the appearances of bread and wine.

Does the divine indwelling of the Trinity, discussed in Chapter 3, render Christ's real presence in the Eucharist superfluous? No, because each represents a different type of presence. In the indwelling the three divine Persons are present in the soul, but the Second Person is present only in his divinity and not with his human nature. In addition, since the Trinity dwells in our soul and the soul is present in every part of our being, the divine indwelling affects our entire substance whereas Christ's real presence in the Eucharist is localized by the accidents or properties of the bread and wine. The Eucharistic presence disappears as the accidents of bread and wine are absorbed in our body. The divine indwelling presence unites us with God while the Eucharist increases that union, restores it, repairs any loss of fervor, and sometimes causes delight. Aquinas summarizes the effects of the Eucharist as "to work a certain transformation of ourselves into Christ."[19] Unlike ordinary food which becomes part of us, the Eucharist is different, as St Albert the Great noted: "Since the power of this heavenly bread incomparably exceeds that of those who receive it, it changes them into itself."[20]

The gift of ourselves

The major parts of the Eucharistic liturgy correspond in a general way to the purgative, illuminative, and unitive stages of the spiritual life—a subject we will consider in Chapter 7. At the beginning of the Mass we acknowledge the truth about ourselves as sinners and our need for God's life-giving forgiveness; in the Liturgy of the Word our minds are illumined and our hearts are moved as we recall the great events of salvation history which are being renewed in us; in the reception of Holy Communion we are united sacramentally to the Lord.

Unfortunately, a certain weakness in post-Conciliar catechesis has resulted in wide-spread ignorance regarding the meaning of the Eucharist. To some people the Eucharist seems like a disconnected addendum to the Liturgy of the Word at which we are only spectators. Christ becomes present on the altar, but many do not understand the reason for his being there.

A starting point for a renewed understanding of the Eucharist is our re-discovery of the central action of offering ourselves to the Father in union with Christ and in his Spirit every time we participate at Mass. We are already united with Christ through baptism and the divine indwelling of the Trinity and the gift of self to God in the Eucharist increases that union. This gift, following the example of Jesus, is at the very heart of the Good News and reflects the inner life of the Trinity where the Father and the Son are completely oriented to the Other in love and mutual self-giving. Jesus' words, "For those who want to save their life will lose it, and those who lose their life for my sake will save it" (Lk. 9.24) reflect the core truth about human existence which, in turn, mirrors the interrelationship among the three divine Persons of the Trinity. The Constitution on the Sacred Liturgy, *Sacrosanctum Concilium*, of the Second Vatican Council, stresses the life-giving importance of self-offering at Mass: "Christ's faithful, when present at this mystery of faith, should not be there as strangers or silent spectators; on the contrary, through a good understanding of the rites and prayers they should take part in the sacred action conscious of what they are doing, with devotion and full collaboration. They should be instructed by God's word and be nourished at the table of the Lord's body; they should give thanks to God; by offering the Immaculate Victim, not only through the hands of the priest, but also with him, *they should learn also to offer themselves*; through Christ the Mediator, they should be drawn day by day into ever more perfect union with God and with each other, so that finally God may be all in all."[21]

Prior to the action of self-offering, however, we should strive—with God's help—to empty ourselves of all falsehood, doubt, selfishness, and anything that is contrary to Love. This *kenosis* or self-emptying is what Jesus did in terms of his divine prerogatives as the Son of God when he came among us as a man. The spiritual life is not so much a matter of our doing anything but rather of making space for God to do something in us. Through renunciation we can choose those areas of our lives that we want to work on, but God will also do his own removing of old securities. One by one he may take away the things we value until our hands are empty. Only with empty hands—freed from false loves and attachments—can we then receive more fully the gift of his divine life.

Our participation in the Eucharist is the most perfect act of divine adoptive filiation because in the liturgy we are joined with Christ, the perfect Son of the Father, in his continual act of pure self-offering and loving obedience to the Father. United with the Son, the Father loves us in Christ. The attitude of self-offering to God with Christ is beautifully encapsulated in the famous *Suscipe* often attributed to St Ignatius of Loyola: "Take Lord, and receive all my liberty, my memory, my understanding, and my entire will—all that I have and call my own. You have given it all to me. To you, Lord, I return it. Everything is yours; do with it what you will. Give me only your love and your grace. That is enough for me."[22]

Assimilation into Christ

The more Christ dwells in us, the more we are united to him and the more he floods us, through the instrument of his sacred humanity, with his own divine life. To receive the Body and Blood of Christ means to receive Christ's whole life. The real presence of Christ in the Eucharist is not for the sake of just being present among us in some static way but reflects his desire to unite himself with us and to bring us to the bosom of the Father who will share his wealth with us. St John Chrysostom imagines Christ in the Eucharist saying: "I have again descended to earth, not simply to be present among you but to embrace you. I leave myself as food for you and I allow myself to be assimilated until our oneness and togetherness are truly perfect. Persons united together maintain their individuality, but I become totally one with you. In the end, I do not want anything to come between us; this only I desire: to be one with you."[23]

Raymond of Capua records that whenever Catherine of Siena received Holy Communion (and she desired to do so everyday), "she felt her soul enter into God, and God into her soul, in the same way as a fish in the sea is in the water, and the water is in the fish. All drawn in and gripped by God, she could barely totter home."[24] Nicholas Cabasilas, a fourteenth-century Orthodox mystic, wrote that in Communion "Christ is transfused into us and merges with us, changing us and transforming us in him, like a drop of water poured into an endless sea of fragrant unguent. The effects of this unction on those who receive it are myriad: it does not just limit itself to simply perfuming, and neither to letting them just breathe in its fragrance; it transforms their very substance into the fragrance of the unction which was given up for us: 'We are the aroma of Christ' (2 Cor 2:15)."[25]

We should not forget that union with Christ also means union with all those in whom Christ lives—including our deceased loved ones. This is the Communion of Saints. As Benedict XVI says, "I cannot possess Christ just for myself; I can belong to him only in union with all those who have become, or will become, his own. Communion draws me out of myself towards him and, thus, towards unity with all Christians."[26]

"Let us rejoice and give thanks," notes St Augustine, "that we have become not only Christians *but Christ himself*."[27]

It gives delight

Aquinas mentions several effects of the Eucharist, one of which is "to give delight."[28] Just as material bread is pleasant to taste, the Eucharistic bread is sweet to the faithful soul. Catherine, whenever she received Communion, would go into ecstasy and become completely impervious to her surroundings for 2 or 3 hours. St Symeon the New Theologian compares ecstasy to the experience of someone born in a dark prison with only a single candle for light and who, one day, through a crack in the wall, suddenly catches a glimpse of the landscape bathed in sunlight.[29]

The desire for experience is uppermost in the minds of many people today. But, as we noted before, deifying grace cannot be experienced directly although God may allow us to experience its effects. The presence of deifying grace is manifested by the fruits of the Holy Spirit and the Beatitudes. Growth in the Spirit, as well as mystical experiences, are not psychological phenomena but rather *ontological* realities, that is, they pertain to our being. Growth in the spiritual life is often slow, gradual and for the most part imperceptible just as the effects of drugs for physical ailments sometimes are. Yet, believers sense that because of Christ, they are very different and better than they would have been otherwise.

St Bonaventure, on the other hand, insisted that we should feel something of the effects of the Lord's presence when we receive Holy Communion: "If after Holy Communion you do not feel a certain spiritual refreshment, it is no small indication of spiritual sickness or death. What if you apply fire to wood and it does not ignite? What if you have honey on your tongue, and yet you do not taste its sweetness? Then do not doubt that this is a most certain sign of ill health."[30] The current preacher to the papal household, Raniero Cantalamessa, OFMCap, says that, "Every Communion should end in an ecstasy if by ecstasy we do not mean the extraordinary but accidental phenomena sometimes experienced by the mystics, but simply the 'getting out' of oneself (which is what the word literally means), the fact that 'it is no longer I that live, but Christ lives in me.'"[31]

"I don't get anything out of the Mass"

Why is it that reception of Holy Communion may seem to make no difference in our lives? Perhaps the single most important reason is the need for reconciliation with God through the sacrament of confession. Other factors may include the absence of *desire* for union with the Lord and a lack of preparation for reception of the Sacrament. The *Catechism* says that the sacraments "bear fruit in those who receive them with the required dispositions."[32] These dispositions or right attitudes, considered negatively, are unmortified passions, disordered affections, and attachments to created goods (things, other persons, ourselves), and our habitual faults or venial sins. Marmion points out that attachment to venial sin is often an overlooked obstacle to spiritual growth: "To remain attached to venial sin, to deliberate imperfections, to willful negligences, and premeditated infidelities, all these things cannot fail to impede our Lord's action when He comes to us. If we desire the perfection of this union we ought not to bargain with Christ for our heart's liberty, nor reserve any place, however small, for creatures loved for their own sake. We should empty ourselves of self, disengage ourselves from creatures, aspire after the perfect coming of Christ's Kingdom within us by the submission of all our being to His Gospel and to the action of His Spirit."[33]

Considered positively, Marmion identifies the general disposition of "the total gift, frequently renewed, of ourselves in Jesus Christ."[34] Blessed John Paul II identifies four specific dispositions which result from devout participation in the Eucharistic celebration: gratitude for heavenly benefits received, an attitude of self-offering, charity, and the yearning to contemplate and bow in adoration before Christ who is really present under the Eucharistic species.[35]

The positive dispositions required for a fruitful reception of the Eucharist can be supported by practices such as frequent confession, daily private prayer, *lectio divina*, or the spiritual reading of a text from Scripture (such as a passage from one of the readings for the Mass of the day), and a vital devotional life which includes Eucharistic adoration. In the life of St Francis de Sales, a fervent disposition to receive Christ in Communion was achieved by making every action of the day a preparation for his self-offering in the Eucharist such that when asked the reason for his conduct he would reply, "I am preparing myself to celebrate Mass."[36]

⚑

Prayer for Union with God

I pray for this, I desire this, that I may be completely united to You
and may withdraw my heart from all created things,
learning to relish the celestial and the eternal
through Holy Communion and the frequent celebration of Mass.
Ah Lord God, when shall I be completely united to You and
absorbed by You,

with self utterly forgotten? You in me and I in You?
Grant that we may remain so together.[37]

Thomas à Kempis

Notes

1 Vladimir Lossky, *The Mystical Theology of the Eastern Church* (Crestwood, NY: St. Vladimir's Seminary Press, 1976), pp.178–79.

2 Joseph Ratzinger, *Jesus of Nazareth: From the Baptism in the Jordan to the Transfiguration*, (San Francisco, CA: Ignatius Press, 2008), p. 47.

3 Ibid., pp. 46–47.

4 See *CCC*, 567, 865. Lk. 7.21: "For lo, the kingdom of God is within you" (Duoay-Rheims).

5 Bernard D. Green, SDS, *Christian Spirituality and Human Development. A Philosophical and Psychological Inquiry* (Tempe, AZ: Institute for the Study of Catholic Faith and Life, 2009), p. 120.

6 Second Vatican Council, "Dogmatic Constitution on the Church," *Lumen gentium* (November 21, 1964), §§3 and 5, in *Vatican Council II. The Conciliar and Post Conciliar Documents* (ed. Austin Flannery, OP; vol. 1; Northport, NY: Costello, 1975), pp. 351, 353.

7 Dorotheus of Gaza, *Instructions* (SC 92, 286) quoted in Clément, *The Roots of Christian Mysticism*, p. 272.

8 Clément, *The Roots of Christian Mysticism*, p. 95.

9 Arintero, *The Mystical Evolution* (vol. 1), p. 11.

10 Second Vatican Council, "Dogmatic Constitution on the Church," *Lumen gentium*, §16, p. 367.

11 T. S. Eliot, "Choruses from 'The Rock'," in T. S. Eliot, *The Complete Poems and Plays 1909–1950* (New York: Harcourt, 1971), p. 106.

12 Jacques Philippe, *Time for God* (New York: Scepter, 2008), p. 77.

13 Ronald Rolheiser, *The Holy Longing. The Search for a Christian Spirituality* (New York: Image Doubleday, 1999), p. 137.

14 *ST* III, q. 62, a. 6.

15 *ST* III, q. 73, a. 3.

16 Bernard D. Green, SDS, *The Humility of God. Reflections on the Importance of the Trinity in Christian Experience* (Tempe, AZ: Institute for the Study of Catholic Faith and Life, 2009), p. 12.

17 Second Vatican Council, "Dogmatic Constitution on the Church," *Lumen Gentium*, §11, p. 362.

18 Aquinas, *In Sent. IV*, dist. 12, a. 1, q. 2 quoted in Arintero, *The Mystical Evolution* (vol. 1), p. 321.

19 Aquinas, *In Sent. IV*, dist. 12, a. 2, q. 1 quoted in Marmion, *Christ the Life of the Soul*, p. 265.

20 Albert the Great, *In IV Sent.*, dist. 9, a.4, ad Ium quoted in Arintero, *The Mystical Evolution* (vol. 1), p. 332.

21 Second Vatican Council, "The Constitution on the Sacred Liturgy," *Sacrosanctum concilium* (December 4, 1963), §48, italics mine, in *Vatican Council II. The Conciliar and Post Conciliar Documents* (ed. Austin Flannery, OP; vol. 1; Northport, NY: Costello, 1975), pp. 16–17. The restoration of the ancient offertory procession in the Mass at which the faithful bring forward the gifts of bread and wine, representing the gift of themselves, puts in relief this important aspect of Eucharistic participation.

22 Ignatius of Loyola, "Contemplation to Gain Love," in *The Spiritual Exercises of St. Ignatius of Loyola* (trans. Elder Mullan; New York: Kennedy, 1914), p. 120. Ignatius did not write the prayer but he cites it.

23 John Chrysostom, *In epistulam I ad Timotheum*, 15, 4; PG 62, 586. See John Chrysostom, *The Homilies of St. John Chrysostom on the Epistles of St. Paul the Apostle to Timothy, Titus and Philemon* (trans. members of the English Church; Oxford: Parker, MDCCXLIII), pp. 139–40.

24 Raymond of Capua, *The Life of Catherine of Siena* (trans. Kearns), §192, pp. 183–84.

25 Nicholas Cabasilas, *The Life in Christ*, IV, 3; PG 150, 593 quoted in Raniero Cantalamessa, OFMCap, *The Eucharist, Our Sanctification* (Collegeville, MN: Liturgical Press, 1993), p. 31.

26 Pope Benedict XVI, "Encyclical on the Love of God," *Deus caritas est* (December 25, 2005), §13, at the Holy See, www.vatican.va.

27 Augustine of Hippo, *In Jo. ev*, 21, 8; PL 35, 1568 quoted in CCC, 795.

28 *ST* III, q. 79, a. 1.

29 Symeon the New Theologian, Homily 45, 10, quoted in Lossky, *The Mystical Theology*, p. 209.

30 Bonaventure, *De preparatione ad Missam* quoted in Arintero, *The Mystical Evolution* (vol. 1), 339 note.

31 Cantalamessa, *The Eucharist*, p. 31.

32 CCC, 1131.

33 Marmion, *Christ the Life of the Soul*, p. 270.

34 Ibid., p. 272.

35 Papa Giovanni Paulo II, Angelus (1 julio 1990) at the Holy See, www.vatican.va.

36 Marmion, *Christ in His Mysteries*, p. 73.

37 Thomas à Kempis, *The Imitation of Christ* (trans. William C. Creasy; Notre Dame, IN: Ave Maria Press, 1989) Book. 4, ch. 13, pp. 150–51.

6

Prayer

*For me, prayer is a surge of the heart; it is a
simple look turned toward heaven,
it is a cry of recognition and of love,
embracing both trial and joy.*[1]

ST THÉRÈSE OF LISIEUX

Prayer, like the sacraments, is also a channel through which God
shares his divine life with us. Christian prayer is essentially *filial*
prayer, the conversation of a loving son or daughter with the
heavenly Father. The classic definition of prayer is that of St John
Damascene (d. 749): "Prayer is the raising of the mind and heart to
God."[2]

Prayer is a response to the divine indwelling and manifests the
presence of the theological virtue of hope. We do not turn to prayer
unless we have hope. Another source of prayer is actual grace, that
intermittent flare of divine life which acts on our minds and hearts
as illuminations and inspirations. The *Catechism* says beautifully:
"Prayer restores man to God's likeness."[3] It is helpful to have a set
period of time every day for prayer and to stick to it unfailingly.
In the beginning, try meditating for just 10 or 15 minutes. Time
spent with God in prayer is never wasted. Prayer is possible even if
one has committed a serious sin; the theological virtue of charity,
however, would now be absent, but faith and hope remain albeit in
a somewhat lifeless way. Our gaze on God has become dull and our
love has grown cold. Christ is no longer the beloved friend he once

was but is more like a stranger seen from a distance. It is not God who has withdrawn but we who have withdrawn from him.

Christian tradition recognizes three expressions of prayer: *vocal prayer, meditation, and contemplation.* Vocal prayer and meditation are means to an end: contemplation. Everyone is called to contemplation or infused prayer. In the first two types of prayer, *we* raise our minds and hearts to God in response to grace; in contemplation, *God* raises our minds and hearts to him.

Vocal prayer

Vocal prayer is prayer with words, either spoken or unspoken. The *Catechism* identifies five forms of vocal prayer: blessing and adoration, prayer of petition, intercession, thanksgiving, and praise. Many people, however, think of prayer only in terms of petition and intercession. Vocal prayer should never be disparaged since we are bodily creatures who most often communicate through words. Our Lord encouraged prayer of petition when he taught us to pray, "Give us our daily bread." When we ask God for something we are acknowledging our dependence on him and so we honor him. It is in vocal prayer that we speak with God.

The greatest vocal prayer after the Lord's Prayer is the Church's Liturgy of the Hours which all the baptized are encouraged to pray at least in part and which priests and consecrated persons such as monks and nuns have committed themselves to pray. Five times of prayer daily are specified consisting of the Psalms, canticles from the Old and New Testaments, and readings from Scripture and the Church Fathers. A place of honor is given to the Hours because the Psalms are the prayers of Jesus himself and therefore express the words and sentiments of the One who, in his human nature, was supremely and uniquely deified.

When we begin praying for the first time, our communication with God is most often entirely on our part. We speak and God listens in silence. It would be futile for God to say much at this point because his inner communications with us always pertain to the soul's deification or union with him which most beginners would not understand.[4] It is as if God is speaking a divine language on a higher frequency that is unintelligible to us, but which the

Holy Spirit will teach us if we are open, desire it, and persevere. The beginner at this point has only a dim perception of self and of God and what he or she truly needs.

As already stated, one form of vocal prayer is *prayer of petition* and it is to this that we now turn. God wants us to pray for spiritual and material things, and in that order. As Aquinas says, "Temporal things we may ask God to grant us in so far as they are expedient to our salvation."[5] Prayers of petition are effective not because they change God's plan but because they are part of it. Providence includes prayer as one of the causes of things. And, as Herbert McCabe says, prayer "is not a matter of bringing God around to our way of thinking but a matter of God bringing *us* around to his way of thinking, changing our minds to what we really need, paying attention to what he has given, recognizing his presence everywhere, loving him and thanking him as our loving Father."[6] We pray not in order to dispose God to give us something but to dispose ourselves to receive what it is he wants to give.

In his commentary on the Sermon on the Mount, St Augustine asks rhetorically why we should pray if God already knows what it is we want. He answers that "prayer clears and cleanses our heart, and makes it more capable of receiving the divine gifts which are spiritually infused into us."[7] Often we know only what we *want* but it is God who knows what we truly *need*. "Your heavenly Father knows all that you need" (Mt. 6.31).[8] We should persevere in prayer because it disposes us to receive what it is we need—which often is quite different from what we want. Prayer arouses humility and hope because it reminds us of our dependence upon God.

Aquinas says that God always gives us what we ask for in prayer providing it is necessary for our salvation.[9] Every prayer that is prompted by the Holy Spirit asks for what is necessary for our salvation. When Jesus said, "Whatever you ask for in prayer, believe that you have received it, and it will be yours" (Mk 11.24), he was speaking of authentic prayer made in the Spirit. We should, therefore, ask God to help us pray for what is pleasing to him. As Paul says, "the Spirit helps us in our weakness; for we do not know how to pray as we ought" (Rom. 8.26). The Spirit is the advocate (Jn 14.16) who stands at our side and formulates a higher request than the one we perhaps had in mind. This is why the Spirit is called the "interior master of Christian prayer."[10]

When God does not give us what we asked for "he is giving us a greater gift, inviting us to grow a little, to realize that we actually *want* these more important things," McCabe says. "The answer he's given is just a little bigger than what we first asked for, and it can be very disturbing and painful to adjust to a new understanding of ourselves and our desires."[11] Augustine says that our prayers are "mercifully heard, and mercifully not heard. For the physician knows better than the sick man what is good for the disease."[12] In heaven we shall praise and thank God for *not* giving us what we had asked for. We pray not so much to get something as to become someone—*imago Christi*, images of Christ. God answers every prayer with the gift of his deifying presence and friendship.

Meditation

As we persevere in vocal prayer the Lord begins to enlighten our intellects to what is true and to excite our wills to what is good although at this point we are more interested in material and natural things than spiritual ones. The more we strip ourselves of vice, as St Catherine says, the more the theological virtues of faith, hope, and charity will increase in us. Gradually our desire for only material things decreases. In the silence we become aware of God's presence, beckoning us to come near and simply be there with him in all of our nakedness without any expectation of reward or experience. God may subtly begin his communication with us and, perhaps for the first time, we may begin to understand him.

Meditation engages thought, imagination, emotion, and desire such that the theological virtues gradually elevate our intellects and wills.[13] Because we are not pure spirits like the angels, the acts of our intellect depend on the senses and our imagination. Therefore, as human beings we must have some image in mind. Jesus Christ is *the* "image of the invisible God" (Col. 1.15) and the events of his life and his words, as found in the Gospels, provide the best object for meditation, as Jacques Philippe says: "Every aspect of his humanity, each of his characteristics, even the smallest and most hidden, each of his words, deeds, and gestures, every stage of his life from his conception in Mary's womb to his Ascension, brings us into communion with God the Father if we receive it in faith.

By exploring his humanity like a piece of land that belongs to us, going through it like a book written especially for us, making it our own in faith and love, we grow steadily in communion with the inaccessible, unfathomable mystery of God." [14]

Meditation can be aided by the use of good religious art such as icons and reproductions of Christ and Mary by the great masters. Candles and incense can also be helpful. The ideal place to pray is before the Blessed Sacrament in a church or chapel, but we can pray anywhere including our room. As Jesus says: "Whenever you pray, go into your room" (Mt. 6.6). Teresa of Avila, in her autobiography, recommends the following simple form of meditation: "We can picture ourselves standing in front of Christ, and arouse in ourselves the liveliest sentiments of love for his Sacred Humanity; live in his presence, talk to him, ask him for the things we need, tell him about the things that are making us suffer, share our joys with him instead of letting them drive him from our thoughts; without looking for well-turned phrases in our prayers, but finding the words that express our desires and needs. This is an excellent way of making very rapid progress; those who make this effort to live in his precious company so as to profit greatly from it and experience real love for our Lord, to whom we owe so much—those are souls I consider to be very advanced." [15]

What happens in meditation is essentially a gradual union of our humanity with the sacred humanity of Jesus Christ, that is, our minds and hearts become more like his and we slowly adopt his way of thinking and outlook. We are introduced to God's way of judging things and are invited to leave behind our former way. This is what St Paul meant when he said, "Let the same mind be in you that was in Christ Jesus" (Phil. 2.5). We begin to see how different we are from him and sense the importance of changing. We become sensitive to the presence of God and, as hope increases, the more we come to trust him to give us what we truly need and not what we had merely wanted or prayed for. God is now doing more of the "speaking"—and this may very well be just an awareness of his presence—and we are growing in our understanding of his "language."

One of the most revered forms of meditation is the ancient *Jesus Prayer*, so much cherished in the Eastern Church: "Lord Jesus Christ, Son of the Living God, have mercy on me, a sinner" (or variations of this) repeated slowly hundreds of times. The charming nineteenth-century work *The Way of a Pilgrim* is the memoirs of a wandering Russian who grew in holiness through the faithful recitation of the prayer.

A popular and ancient form of meditation which originated in the monastic movement is *lectio divina* or the sacred reading of a text from Scripture. Benedict XVI has encouraged this form of prayer for everyone. It involves a slow and careful reading of a short text, such as one of the readings for Mass, and then interiorizing it, and applying it to ourselves. Imagination comes into play and use is made of allegorical interpretations of Bible passages. Because reading Scripture is so important in Christian life, this method of meditation is highly recommended.

Another form of meditation that is well-known and beloved by many is the *Rosary* of the Blessed Virgin Mary which has spiritually nourished countless men and women for centuries. This prayer consists of 150 or 200 angelic salutations ("Hail Mary . . .") and the Lord's Prayer and the *Gloria Patri* recited while meditating on one of the 15 or 20 mysteries or events in the life of Christ and Mary. The Rosary itself is a circular chain or cord of beads with a medal and crucifix attached. In 2002, Pope John Paul II added an optional five decades called "The Luminous Mysteries." In the Rosary, Mary invites us to see her Son through her eyes. Thousands of meditations on the mysteries of the Rosary have been written over the centuries. For those who are beginning to pray the Rosary, the meditations of Blessed John XXIII in his *Journal of a Soul* are recommended.

Now begins—if one perseveres in prayer—what some mystics have referred to as divine delicate touches. However, because our sensitivity to spiritual things is still somewhat dull, we are often not aware of what is happening. Of course all growth in the spiritual life is God's doing and not ours and it is not really important whether or not we are conscious of what is happening. God helps to dispose us and opens us to his action in our lives. As the activity of God on the soul increases our own mental activity diminishes. We are invited by God to leave behind images, concepts, and words and to approach his essence in a state of spiritual poverty. At this point we are ushered into the presence of God in a completely new way. All of this, keep in mind, is the normal flowering of baptismal grace—faith, hope, and charity crowned by the Gifts of the Holy Spirit—to which all the baptized are called.

Meditation is of great value, the *Catechism* tells us, "but Christian prayer should go further: to the knowledge of the love of the Lord Jesus, to union with him."[16]

Contemplation

Spiritual writers speak differently of contemplation and there is no single definition of this expression of prayer. Following the lines of the *Catechism*, we prefer to speak of contemplation as *infused prayer* in which we are raised by God into the divine life. It is union with the prayer of Christ and happens when the Gifts of the Holy Spirit are actuated. We now experience an ever-increasing union of our mind and heart with God's and at this point the mystics (and many are lay people) often use the word "taste" to describe their encounter with the divine. Compared to vocal prayer and meditation, this type of prayer is passive. In meditation, we grow in union with the humanity of Christ; in contemplation we grow in union with his divinity. It is now God who prays *in* us.

The ultimate purpose of prayer is God's self-communication with us. "Prayer," Jacques Philippe says in his marvelous book on prayer *Time for God*, "now becomes a deep outpouring of love, sometimes perceptible and sometimes not, in which God and the soul give themselves to one another. [. . .] God pours himself into the soul and the soul pours itself into God by the working of the Holy Spirit in our souls."[17] Contemplation is a preparation for the eternal contemplation of the beatific vision in heaven which is the end or purpose of human life. "The delight of contemplation," Aquinas says, "surpasses all human delight."[18] Through prayer we pass through the humanity of Christ to God: "I am the way. . . . No one comes to the Father except through me" (Jn 14.6). All Christian prayer is traditionally addressed *to the Father*, *through the Son* (we are members of his Body by baptism), *in the Spirit* (the Spirit of Jesus is sent to unite us to God).

St Paul's experience of being "caught up to the third heaven," described in 2 Cor. 12.2–6, is interpreted in Catholic tradition as a mystical experience. Paul recounts that he "heard things that are not to be told," that is, that which could not be put into words. However, nowhere in Paul's letters does he suggest that such an experience is a goal of Christian life. Rather, he seems to regard what happened as a divine ratification of his being an apostle, although not one of the original Twelve. Catholicism teaches that extraordinary phenomena in prayer should never be sought for their own sake.

As the letters of Blessed Mother Teresa of Calcutta to her spiritual directors have revealed, infused prayer or contemplation is not a continuous experience of consolations and delight. As God draws us closer to himself we are painfully despoiled of our dissimilarities and any vestigial resistance to the Divine. But Mother Teresa was even thankful for this. In a letter to her spiritual director, she wrote: "I have no words to express the depth of the darkness. In spite of it all—I am His little one—and I love Him—not for what He gives— but for what he takes."[19] This is a type of dark night which many mystics have experienced and which St John of the Cross spoke of in *Dark Night of the Soul*.

🜨

I Asked God for Strength

Prayer said to have been found in the pocket
of an unknown Confederate soldier who died on the battlefield.

I asked God for strength, that I might achieve;
I was made weak, that I might humbly learn to obey.
I asked for health, that I might do greater things;
I was given infirmity, that I might do better things.
I asked for riches, that I might be happy;
I was given poverty, that I might be wise.
I asked for power, that I might have the praise of men;
I was given weakness, that I might feel the need of God.
I asked for all things, that I might enjoy life;
I was given life, that I might enjoy all things.
I received nothing that I asked for
– but everything that I had hoped for;
Almost despite myself, my unspoken prayers were answered.
I am, among all people, most richly blessed.

Notes

1 Thérèse of Lisieux, *Manuscrits Autobiographiques*, C 25r, quoted in CCC before 2559. Cf. Thérèse of Lisieux, *Story of a Soul*, p. 242.
2 John Damascene, *De fide orth.* 3, 24; PG 94, 1089C quoted in CCC, 2559.
3 CCC, 2572.
4 See Edward Leen, CSSp, *Progress through Mental Prayer* (New York: Sheed and Ward, 1935), p. 60.
5 *ST* II-II, q. 83, a. 6, ad 4.
6 Herbert McCabe, OP, *God, Christ and Us* (New York: Continuum, 2005), pp. 6–7.
7 Augustine of Hippo. *Commentary on the Lord's Sermon on the Mount with Seventeen Related Sermons* (trans. Denis J. Kavanaugh, OSA; The Fathers of the Church. A New Translation; New York: Fathers of the Church, 1951), p. 121.
8 New American Bible.
9 *ST* II-II, q. 83, a. 15.
10 CCC, 2671.
11 McCabe, *God, Christ and Us*, p. 9.
12 Augustine of Hippo, *Liber. Sentent. Prosperi Sent. ccxii* quoted in *ST* II-II, 83, 15, 2.
13 CCC, 2708.
14 Philippe, *Time for God*, p. 58.
15 Teresea of Avila, *Life*, ch. 12, translation in Jacques Phillipe, *Time for God*, p. 61.
16 CCC, 2708.
17 Philippe, *Time for God*, p. 70.
18 *ST* II-II, q. 180, a. 7.
19 Mother Teresa, *Come Be My Light. The Private Writings of the* "Saint of Calcutta" (ed. with commentary by Brian Kolodiejchuk, MC; New York: Image Doubleday, 2007), p. 172.

7

Growing in grace

*And since I in the beginning created man to
my own image and likeness,
and afterwards took your image on myself
by assuming human nature,
it is always my endeavor, in so far as you are fit for it,
to intensify that likeness between me and you.*[1]

THE ETERNAL FATHER TO ST CATHERINE OF SIENA

Just as the human body is meant to grow the same is true of our
spiritual lives. In the second letter of Peter (3.18), for example, we
are extolled to grow in grace. St Paul alludes to spiritual growth
when he criticizes the Corinthians for being "infants in Christ"
(1 Cor. 3.1) and when he exhorts the Ephesians to grow "to the
measure of the full stature of Christ" (Eph. 4.13), adding that "we
must grow up in every way into him who is the head, into Christ"
(4.15). In his letter to the Galatians (4.19) he compares himself to a
pregnant woman in the pangs of childbirth "until Christ is formed
in you."

For centuries Christians have been interested in demarcating
stages of the spiritual life. The Fathers and theologians distinguish
generally three stages of spiritual growth: the state of beginners,
those making progress, and the perfect. Pseudo-Dionysius's division
of the spiritual life into the purgative, illuminative, and unitive
ways is the most well-known. The value of these expositions is in
enabling us to identify the quality of our love of God and neighbor

and imparting to us an awareness of higher forms of love to which we are called and of which we may have never known. *Ignoti nulla cupido*: those who do not know of something have no desire for it. In the past the impression was sometimes given that the spiritual life is like moving mechanically from one phase to the next as if the stages were squares on a Monopoly board. A better image of the spiritual life is that of an upward spiral which continuously passes through the same stages or phases of purgation, illumination, and union but on a higher level of re-integration and deification.

Here Catholic teaching differs from classical Protestantism which sees grace essentially as God's acceptance and forgiveness instead of a transforming energy or participation in the divine life. Therefore, many of our Protestant brothers and sisters have traditionally not regarded the spiritual life as a journey toward God or in terms of stages of growth in one's spiritual likeness to Christ.

Of course, occasional regression is often part of the spiritual life and when this happens we should not succumb to discouragement. John Paul II once said, "Christian holiness does not mean being sinless, but rather it means struggling not to give in and always getting up after every fall."[2] We may find ourselves struggling with the same issues in life over and over again, although at a higher level than before. The Evil One, as well as our own wounded human spirit, may tempt us to think that no progress is being made, that our desire to grow and change is futile, that we will always be the same and that we should just give up. At such times we would do well to remember Peter's admonition: "Like a roaring lion your adversary the devil prowls around, looking for someone to devour. Resist him, steadfast in your faith" (1 Pt 5.8–9).

Spiritual growth as an ever-greater participation in the divine life is certainly an adventure but it is seldom easy or fun since it entails going the painful way of the Cross with Christ, a way of radical trust in God and renunciation of old securities. As Jesus said, "How hard it is to enter the kingdom of God!" (Mk 10.24). Bernard Green makes the following observation: "To grow spiritually demands struggle. We have to struggle against many attitudes and habits that block the capacity to change in life-giving ways. Unlike many people today who have an optimistic and rather superficial idea of what growth is and the ease with which it can be accomplished, I . . . suggest that there are major forces within us which block the growth process and that meeting and overcoming these forces

is far from easy. However, overcoming these forces is at the heart
of spiritual growth and development. Many people, I suspect,
are disappointed in their efforts to grow spiritually because they
underestimate the power of the forces involved."[3]

Catherine of Siena

The bulk of the *Dialogue* of Catherine of Siena (1347–80)
concerns the stages of the spiritual life. Her thought stays close
to the Gospel and is very practical. The *Dialogue*, which is the
account of a conversation between God and Catherine, is thought
to have been written between 1377 and 1378. In the work she
asks a few questions and the eternal Father replies at length. The
book is a spiritual classic although it demands some patience and
perseverance on the part of the reader owing to the inconsistency
of terminology, overlapping arguments, interruptions, and
repetitions owing to the fact that Catherine dictated the book
in installments to disciple-secretaries while she was in a mystical
state. There are, nonetheless, many nuggets of gold buried in the
Dialogue which make reading it worthwhile. In addition to the
Dialogue, we have Catherine's 381 letters and 26 prayers, all of
which have been translated in English. The letters are treatises on
the spiritual life and resemble spiritual conferences or sermons
coming from the depths of her great humanity. It is in the letters
that we come to know Catherine personally and sense her
presence.

Catherine's theological language is that of images—homey
images drawn from her daily life. She compares the soul to a
house, a city, and a vineyard. The Church she compares to a wine
cellar (a nice Italian analogy!) and the pope to the cellar master.
She compares baptism to a lamp. She has hundreds of images to
illustrate the various articles of faith. In a certain sense, she could
be called a doctrinal mystical theologian, although as a mystic she
did not explore the truths of faith in an exclusively intellectual
way but rather as someone who had had an encounter with God.
She presents religious truth, therefore, not solely as the result of
reasoning but as the result of an intimately lived experience.[4] As
John Paul II said, hers was a "lived theology."[5]

The bridge of Christ crucified

Catherine's most important image on which she hangs many of her most important teachings is the crucified Christ as a bridge stretching from heaven to earth. The sin of Adam had destroyed the road to heaven, so out of love the eternal Father made of his Son a bridge so that we could approach him and become like him by sharing in his life, joy, and beauty. Catherine frequently reminds us that humanity is made in God's image and likeness, and that God's plan is for the divine likeness in us to increase through grace to the point of ultimate resemblance.

Progress on the bridge is made in stages represented by three stairs (admittedly, stairs on a bridge are hard to imagine) which lead first to the feet of Christ, then to his opened-side, and finally to his mouth. Each of the three stairs represents an increase of one's knowledge and love of God and neighbor. The journey begins with "stripping" oneself of vice and "putting on" virtue. The most important virtue is charity, followed by humility and patience. Patience is the litmus test of whether one really possesses the other two virtues; it is the only virtue, Catherine says, which cannot be faked. When one truly loves God it means that we love what he loves—ourselves and our neighbors. Catherine constantly stresses the role of the neighbor in her spiritual teaching. No one crosses the bridge alone; everyone must have a companion—meaning that we must be in relationship with others and not isolated from them.

Before describing each of Catherine's three stages of spiritual development, let us first look at some of her principle teachings regarding spiritual growth. Spiritual growth is possible because we are made in God's image and likeness—a reality which is meant to be dynamic, not static. Through God's gift of grace and our free cooperation, we are called to be images of Christ by participating in God's own nature and life through deifying grace.

The incentive to pass along the bridge toward God and therefore to become more Christ-like is owing to the attraction of Love emanating from the head of the Christ-Bridge. The eternal Father tells Catherine: "The soul cannot live without love. She always wants to love something because love is the stuff she is made of, and through love I created her."[6] But only that which is greater than ourselves can ever ultimately satisfy us, and only God—not any created thing—is greater. God is love and he attracts us with the hook of his love and we respond. This is Catherine's interpretation of Christ's words: "And I, when I am lifted up from the earth, will draw all people to myself" (Jn 12.32).

Progress on the Christ-Bridge involves the intellect and the will, the chief faculties of God and humanity. But one cannot love God unless he or she first "sees" or knows him as he really is. "One who knows more, loves more," Catherine says.[7] Knowledge of God involves knowing the truth about his radical love as shown by his bleeding and dying on the Cross. Because God is a "holy abyss," knowledge and love of him are wonderfully endless—even in eternal life. Sin, on the other hand, acts like a cataract that prevents us from seeing the truth; it clouds or even blinds the "eye," which is Catherine's image for the intellect and faith. Sin is the result of defective knowledge and disordered desire. It is an over-attachment to finite things: self, other creatures, or material things. Spiritual growth, therefore, is not a matter of more or less violent acts of the will but rather a matter of more knowledge of the truth—or, we might say, a broader perspective of the truth. This principle is typically Thomistic and Dominican.

Catherine, following St Augustine, says that "love transforms one into what one loves."[8] If we love God, we will be transformed into him. Catherine also echoes St Athanasius when she says, "God was made human and humanity was made God."[9] To love sin, however, is to love nothing because sin has no being; it is literally *no-thing*, and to love it is ultimately to be transformed into it.

With these key ideas or principles of Catherine's spiritual thought, let us now look at her teaching on the three stairs or stages of spiritual development on the body of Christ crucified, the Christ-Bridge.

The first stair

Under the bridge of Christ crucified there is a tempestuous river in which are found those who have loved wrongly; it is the abode of sinners. Unless they get out of the river, they will eventually be washed away. Sinners can get out if they pay attention to the worm of conscience sent by God to nibble and awaken them. But, alas, sin has blinded even the worm so that its nibbling is often ineffective. Some of those in the river, however, are awakened and now see the fearful punishments awaiting them because of their sins. They get out of the water and once on the shore they vomit out their sins, symbolic of sacramental confession. Now they are ready to approach the bridge—unless the wind, symbolic of memories of past sins or the fear of suffering, blows them back into the river.

If pilgrim travelers are to ascend the Christ-Bridge they must first lift their feet and put them firmly onto the Cross and Christ's nailed feet. The feet represent one's affections (feelings and desires) which at this point are disordered. Here the pilgrim traveler must remove all inordinate or excessive attachments to persons and other created things, represented by lifting one's feet from the ground, and then putting them on Christ's feet, signifying that our minds and hearts are now centered on his desires. Catherine does not say that we must remove all affections (that would be impossible) but only those that are disordered in that they are held *apart* from God. Every created thing is good, she says, but everything (including marriage and friendship) must be held in God and for God.

At each stop on the body of Christ, Catherine describes the pilgrim traveler's relationship with God using a personal image. At this point he or she is the *mercenary servant* who works for pay, the "pay" being the avoidance of punishment. Servile fear, not love, describes the mercenary servant's relationship with God. He or she does what is right only out of fear. Many go no further than this stage and are often blown back into the river. Servile fear is never enough to bring one to God: "Since fear has to do with punishment, love is not yet perfect in one who is afraid" (1 Jn 4.18).

When our affections and attachments are rectified and centered on Christ, we begin to sense the attraction of Love emanating from the head of the Bridge and, because we are made by Love and for love, we are attracted to it. This attraction reflects an implicit desire to be with God, to be united with him. Gradually our knowledge and love of him increases, especially as we open the eye of the intellect and faith to see the blood of the crucified One which is the undeniable proof of God's love for us. We begin to realize that until now our relationship with God has been borne out of self-interest and has had little to do with genuine love. This selfish self-love causes many to be blown back into the river. Those who persevere, however, are now transformed from mercenary servants into *faithful servants.* Faithful servants do not fear God; they love him—but not perfectly. We now arrive at the second stair on the body of Christ crucified: the opened-side.

The second stair

The faithful servant's love is imperfect for this reason: he or she loves God's gifts more than God himself. These gifts are the joys and consolations, spiritual and material, that God may communicate to them—especially at the beginning of their spiritual journey—and which they of course enjoy and become strongly attached to. Unfortunately, their love is actually little more than disguised selfish self-love. They love God for what they can "get out" of him and they love their neighbor in the same way.

Fortunately, God loves his faithful servants too much to leave them in this condition of imperfect love. He now intervenes by withdrawing all his gifts but without ever actually withdrawing his grace or presence—only the feeling of its effects. They now experience a severe crisis, a "dark night of self-knowledge" and think that God has abandoned them and that there is no longer any advantage in serving him. But there is a purpose behind this crisis: God wants them to see that their love has only been selfish self-love and the necessity of purifying it. "Pain makes [the soul] enter into knowledge of herself," Catherine says.[10] If they persevere, God always returns with his gifts and the pilgrim travelers will have then learned the important lesson that genuine love of God is not shown in serving him for the sake of joys and consolations but in persevering during their absence and especially in times of suffering. Many pilgrim travelers never go this far and are blown back into the river of sin.

As knowledge and love of God increase, the faithful servants undergo yet another transformation—they become the *friends* of God. Many of Catherine's images are scriptural: the mercenary servant is the hireling in Jn 10.12–13, the faithful servant, and the friend are reminiscent of Jn 15.15: "I do not call you servants any longer, because the servant does not know what the master is doing; but I have called you friends, because I have made known to you everything that I have heard from my Father." Pilgrim travelers are now increasingly conscious of being loved.[11] Friendship love is one of excellence and those who possess it serve God in the simple hope of pleasing him.[12] Because their love is perfect, and because all love unites the lover with the beloved, a bond of union emerges between the friend and God.

The friend then arrives at Christ's opened-side where one can look inside and see "the secret of the heart." It is here that we are radically converted (she calls it a "re-baptism") and, to use her words, we "see" and "taste" and "experience" the fire of divine charity.[13] "For that splitting open of his body has made it clear to us that God loves us without measure and wants nothing other than our good."[14] Pilgrim travelers once they become friends of God are on fire with love and no longer walk but run along the Christ-Bridge.

The third stair

We come now to the third stair or stage on the Christ-Bridge where the friend arrives at the mouth of Christ and receives his kiss of peace. This is another image inspired by Scripture: "Let him kiss me with the kisses of his mouth!" (Song 1.2). The war between our disordered will and the divine will has ended and peace ensues. A final transformation occurs at this point: the friend becomes the *son* or *child* of God while remaining a friend. The pilgrim traveler now loves God "most perfectly" with filial love, that is, the love which, seen from the human side, serves God without any self-interest and, seen from God's side, is a love that is stable, not fleeting, and that makes one an heir to the Father's wealth.

The child no longer craves spiritual consolations but glories in suffering for Christ. His or her eyes are fixed on the Giver and not on his gifts, even though God may give them. The child loves its neighbor as much as it loves God and is now also concerned about God's honor and the salvation of souls. Catherine says that the apostolic vista of the pilgrim traveler is dramatically broadened at this point: he or she becomes "an instrument of mediation" and even "another Christ" who undertakes his "office."[15] Given the times in which she lived, this is a daring extension of the apostolate of the non-ordained. This dignity is possible because of humanity's complete re-integration.[16] There is one final task of the most perfect, according to Catherine: to be "attentive . . . to the reform of holy Church."[17] By this she means the moral and spiritual reform of the Church, especially of the clergy and hierarchy.

Catherine surprises us by introducing a "fourth stage of perfect union." This stage is a "fruit that comes from the third stage."[18] Here the pilgrim traveler arrives at the gate at the end of the Christ-Bridge and, as it were, glimpses the other side. (One passes through the gate only at death.) This is a continuation of the unitive stage which began at the third stair. Now the soul experiences intermittently a pledge or foretaste of eternal life which awaits it on the other side. Catherine devotes a considerable amount of space to the fourth stage, but suffice it to say that she uses images pertaining to union, seeing, clothing, or filling to describe it. For example, she describes the union of the soul with God using the image of the soul nursing at the breast of Christ where it drinks the divine milk (an allusion to divine life) and, as Christ tells Catherine, "tastes within itself my divine nature."[19]

At death, the pilgrim traveler passes through the gate and into the peaceful sea, an image of the Godhead. It is at this point that the "gentle loving Word" tells Catherine: "If you should ask me who these souls are, I would answer . . . that they are *another me*."[20]

⇧

And all of us, with unveiled faces,
seeing the glory of the Lord as though reflected in a mirror,
are being transformed into the same image
from one degree of glory to another.

2 Cor. 3.18

Notes

1 Raymond of Capua, *The Life of Catherine of Siena* (trans. Kearns), §111, p. 103. Italics mine.
2 Pope John Paul II, *Go in Peace: A Gift of Enduring Love* (Chicago, IL: University of Loyola Press, 2005), p. 111.
3 Bernard D. Green, SDS, *Death, Sin, and the Gospel* (Tempe, AZ: The Institute for the Study of Catholic Faith and Life, 2006), p. 3.

4   See E. Ancilli and D. de Pablo Maroto, "Caterina da Siena (santa)," *Dizionario Enciclopedico di Spiritualità. Nuova edizione.* (vol. 1; Roma: Città Nuova Editrice, 1990), p. 485.

5   John Paul II, "Apostolic Letter," *Novo Millennio Ineunte* (January 6, 2001), §27 at the Holy See, www.vatican.va.

6   Catherine of Siena, *Dialogue* (trans. Noffke), ch. 51, p. 103.

7   Ibid., ch. 66, p. 126.

8   Ibid., ch. 60, p. 115.

9   Ibid., ch. 15, p. 53.

10 Ibid., ch. 144, p. 302.

11 Kenelm Foster, OP, "St. Catherine's Teaching on Christ," in *Life of the Spirit* 16 (1962), p. 321.

12 See Catherine of Siena, *Dialogue* (trans. Noffke), ch. 136, p. 281.

13 *Ibid.*, ch. 76, p. 140.

14 Letter T253 in Catherine of Siena, *The Letters* (vol. 2; trans. Noffke), p. 423.

15 Catherine of Siena, *Dialogue* (trans. Noffke), ch. 146, p. 307. The section entitled "Divine Providence."

16 Alvaro Grion, OP, *La dottrina di Santa Caterina da Siena* (Brescia: Morcelliana, 1962), p. 174.

17 Catherine of Siena, *Dialogue* (trans. Noffke), ch. 133, pp. 272–73.

18 Ibid., ch. 78, p. 144.

19 Ibid., ch. 96, p. 179.

20 Ibid., ch. 1, p. 26. Italics mine.

8

Peaceful sea

In order to be sought after having been found, God is infinite.[1]
ATTRIBUTED TO ST AUGUSTINE OF HIPPO

The human person is created to share in the divine life of the Trinity but participation in it in this life is partial and imperfect owing to our finite condition as well as to the limitations sin has placed on our minds and hearts. It is only in the afterlife, in heaven, that the definitive deification—*beatitude*—will take place. "Heaven," the *Catechism* says, "is the ultimate end and fulfillment of the deepest human longings, the state of supreme, definitive happiness." Heaven is not a place "but a way of being."[2]

Many people are ambivalent about "going to" heaven owing, in part, to the unimaginative way in which it has often been presented. One writer described heaven as "a vague place of eternal survival, where happiness can become monotonous and where the absence of human passions creates an 'anemic' atmosphere." Heaven is perceived by some as an eternal church service which is, to be frank, eternally boring. Given the false impressions that people have of heaven, some would prefer instead a continuation of life as we know it. But, as Pope Benedict XVI says, to live the present life endlessly would be monotonous and unbearable. It would be a curse.[3]

Eternal life

While the Old Testament speaks of *life* it is only in the New Testament that the words *eternal life* (Greek, *zoe aionios*) appear.

This expression, which is found frequently in the Johannine writings, is the most apt description of the afterlife. Eternal life is the consummation of the divine indwelling of the Trinity. However, John uses the present tense to illustrate that eternal life, which is divine life, begins now: "Very truly, I tell you, anyone who hears my word and believes him who sent me *has* eternal life" (Jn 5.24).

Heaven is an infinitely multi-faceted reality which far surpasses our intellects. Nonetheless, the New Testament speaks of it in four principal ways: the coming of the reign of God, the vision of God, entering into the joy of the Lord, and into God's rest.[4] As we saw in the last chapter, Catherine of Siena compares heaven to being immersed in a divine sea where God is "all in all" (1 Cor. 15.28). Heaven is to "enter into me, the sea of peace," God tells her.[5] Using the same image, Benedict XVI says that heaven is not "an unending succession of days in the calendar . . . but something more like the supreme moment of satisfaction, in which totality embraces us and we embrace totality. . . . It would be like plunging into the ocean of infinite love, a moment in which time—the before and after—no longer exists. We can only attempt to grasp the idea that such a moment is life in the full sense, a plunging ever anew into the vastness of being, in which we are simply overwhelmed with joy."[6]

Jesus said, "Blessed are the pure in heart, for they will see God" (Mt. 5.8) and the Apostle Paul wrote, "For now we see in a mirror, dimly, but then we will see face to face. Now I know only in part; then I will know fully, even as I have been fully known" (1 Cor. 13.12). The face to face vision of God in the afterlife is called the *beatific vision*. (The expression "face of God" is an analogy which means the direct and total manifestation of God.) Undoubtedly it is not apparent to many people why the prospect of contemplating God for all eternity would be something we should look forward to. Descartes, for example, was afraid of getting bored looking at God for 10,000 years. But to see God is to know him and to know God is to love him and, since love unites one with the beloved, it means to be fully transformed into him. "When he is revealed, we will be like him, for we will see him as he is" (1 Jn 3.2). Here we are reminded of Catherine's words: "Love transforms one into what one loves."[7]

But how can we finite human beings ever hope to see God who is Supreme Being and invisible? Did not God tell Moses, "You cannot see my face; for no one shall see me and live" (Exod. 33.20)? And in the New Testament, Paul refers to God as one who "dwells in unapproachable light, whom no one has ever seen or can see" (1 Tim. 6.15–16). Even with the infused virtues and Gifts of the Holy Spirit, God is so infinitely transcendent that we would still be unable to see him. However, as Augustine says, "God is invisible by nature, but *is seen when he wills and as he wills*."[8] "In your light," the Psalmist says to God, "we see light."[9] God gives us the capacity to see him as he is by infusing into the soul a special light which theologians call the *lumen gloriae* or light of glory, a created gift that vastly expands our power of knowing so that, as Benedict XII famously proclaimed centuries ago, the blessed in heaven will "see the divine essence with an intuitive vision and even face to face, without any mediation of any creature by way of object of vision; rather the divine essence immediately manifests itself to them, plainly, clearly and openly, and in this vision [the blessed] enjoy the divine essence."[10] Not only will we see God in his essence, but we will see everyone and everything *in* God. The light of glory is the crowning perfection, the blossom, of the divine indwelling of the Trinity when our souls, like Elijah's chariot of fire, are raised ecstatically into the fullness of divine life.[11] This happens only in the afterlife.

Will we really see God in the *same* way that he sees and knows himself? No. Aquinas says that in seeing God's essence we will know him but not in an exhaustive way or as God knows himself. We could never have a comprehensive knowledge of him. We will fully see God but each in proportion to Christ's presence in us at the time of death. In other words, the beatific vision will be in proportion to the divine indwelling. The blessed will be like vessels of different sizes representing the extent to which the Trinity dwelled within each one at death, yet all are completely filled with divine life. The Church honors Mary under the title "Spiritual Vessel" as the one who was most receptive to the Divine.

Heaven is something that no one in this life has ever experienced but only vaguely glimpsed from afar. Even the greatest mystics— some of whom were thought to have died and then awakened after many hours—acknowledge that their ecstasies were mere foretastes of what is to come. As Paul says, "What no eye has seen, nor ear heard, nor the human heart conceived, what God has prepared for those who love him" (1 Cor. 2.9). Like other mystics, Catherine found it impossible to describe her most profound mystical experiences. "The inmost feeling, the ineffable sweetness and perfect union," she recounts in the *Dialogue*, "you cannot describe it with your tongue, which is a finite thing!"[12]

Nevertheless, the saints and mystics have described these foretastes of heaven as states of happiness and fulfillment which are without the slightest trace of boredom. Catherine speaks of the blessed as being satisfied but never bored, always desirous of more but never experiencing the pain of want, filled with love without suffering or jealousy.[13] Innocenzo Colosio, OP, describes heaven as an experience of "interior surprises" in which there will be "an inextinguishable thirst to enjoy God; this thirst is a continuation of desire. . . . From one satisfied desire there will spring another and then another according to a vital chain."[14] In heaven the Son will reveal ever-new truths about the Father which will give us delight and satisfaction as well as a thirst for more which will not be denied us. Likewise, St Gregory of Nyssa noted that in heaven the soul will experience never ending growth as it continues to desire and possess the Beloved, "never ceasing to raise its sights. . . . Each time its desire is fulfilled the desire for higher realities is engendered."[15] He goes on to say: "At each instant, what is grasped is much greater than what had been grasped before, but, since what we are seeking is unlimited, the end of each discovery becomes the starting point for the discovery of something higher, and the ascent continues."[16] As Catherine says to the eternal Father, "The more the soul possesses you the more she seeks you, and the more she seeks and desires you the more she finds and enjoys you, high eternal fire, abyss of charity!"[17]

Our capacity for receiving will increase endlessly in heaven. Searching for and desiring God, says Bernard of Clairvaux, is infinitely joyful: "Does the consummation of joy bring about the consuming of desire? Rather it is oil poured upon the flames. So it is. Joy will be fulfilled, but there will be no end to desire, and therefore no end to the search. Think, if you can, of this eagerness to see God as not caused by his absence, for he is always present; and think of the desire for God as without fear of failure, for grace is abundantly present."[18]

Heaven is not a solitary individual experience but is a social or communal one. We are united not only with God but also with all the blessed. In heaven, Catherine says, those who shared a special love for each other on earth—as did she and Raymond of Capua— "will love and share with each other even more closely and fully, adding their love to the good of all."[19]

Tempestuous river

"The specificity of Christianity is shown in this conviction of the greatness of man. *Human life is fully serious*," wrote Joseph Ratzinger (the future Benedict XVI) in 1988.[20] The possibility of not attaining heaven is real. To return to Catherine's image, under the bridge of Christ crucified there is a tempestuous river in which sinners are washed away to eternal separation from God.

The *Catechism* affirms the existence of hell: "Immediately after death the souls of those who die in a state of mortal sin descend into hell."[21] It is important to remember that *God sends no one to hell*—he gives us only what we have desired most: the things of God, or the things that are not of God. It is for this reason that the *Catechism* describes hell as the "state of definitive *self-exclusion* from communion with God and the blessed."[22] Theologian Paul O'Callaghan notes that, "Hell is precisely the crystallization and final expression of the unrepentant sinner's innermost conviction: that of wishing to exist and act as if nothing else existed and acted, or better, as if everything that existed fell under his exclusive, despotic dominion."[23] Sinful actions, in and of themselves, are not the cause of anyone going to hell but rather *unrepented* sin. "It is human to sin," Catherine says, "but diabolic to persist in sin."[24]

In hell the damned will be forever separated from God and will experience his unchanging love now as a torment of tremendous remorse. The seventh-century Syrian bishop and theologian Isaac of Nineveh wrote: "As for me, I say that those who are tormented in hell are tormented by the invasion of love. What is there more bitter and more violent than the pains of love? Those who feel that they have sinned against love bear in themselves a damnation much heavier than the most dreaded punishments. The suffering with which sinning against love afflicts the heart is more keenly felt than any other torment. It is absurd to suppose that sinners in hell are deprived of God's love. Love . . . is offered impartially. But by its very power it acts in two ways. It torments sinners, as happens here on earth when we are tormented by the presence of a friend to whom we have been unfaithful. And it gives joy to those who have been faithful. That is what the torment of hell is in my opinion—remorse."[25]

The divine indwelling of the Trinity was absent in the souls of the damned at the time of death. Instead of experiencing the Holy

Spirit as a gentle deifying energy within, it is now like an afflicting external flame as it comes into contact with selfish self-love.

Purgatory

The doctrine of purgatory—a transitional state of purification, healing and liberation for those who died in God's grace and friendship but who are stained by the vestiges of repented sin—was not defined by the Church until the Middle Ages although belief in it is implicit in Scripture and in the practice of early Christians. The Old Testament text most often cited in support of purgatory is 2 Macc. 12.40–45 (Catholic and Orthodox Bible) in which praying for the dead is commended. The essence of the doctrine has also been located in 1 Cor. 3.12–15 where Paul writes: "Now if anyone builds on the foundation with gold, silver, precious stones, wood, hay, straw the work of each builder will become visible, for the Day will disclose it, because it will be revealed with fire, and the fire will test what sort of work each has done. If what has been built on the foundation survives, the builder will receive a reward. If the work is burned up, the builder will suffer loss; the builder will be saved, but only as through fire."

The souls in purgatory, like ourselves, are wayfarers and belong to the Church and the Communion of Saints. As the catacombs in Rome attest, Christians since the earliest times have been moved to pray for the dead so that they might soon pass from purgatory into the joy of beatitude. The custom is preserved in the spiritual works of mercy where we are exhorted "to pray for the living and the dead." Pope St Gregory the Great (d. 604) stated: "We must believe in a cleansing fire before the judgment for certain minor faults."[26]

"New heavens and the new earth"

[May we] be always free from sin and safe from all distress, as we await the blessed hope and the coming of our Savior, Jesus Christ.

ROMAN MISSAL

Every time the Eucharist is celebrated we are reminded of the *Parousia*, the second coming of the Lord Jesus in glory, that is, with his risen and spiritualized humanity. For those in whom Christ dwells, the waiting is confident, hopeful, and filled with expectant joy.

Parousia is a Greek word found in many passages of the New Testament which originally referred to the triumphal entrance of a king or victorious conqueror. When Christ comes again in glory he will raise the bodies of all the dead and re-unite them with their souls. Then, as Scripture and tradition affirm, there will be a second judgment which, unlike the first one immediately after death, will be a social manifestation of God's justice and mercy for all to see. The cosmos—the material universe—will be re-created in such a way that the relationship between creation and Christ will now be one of perfect harmony, similar to what existed in the Garden of Eden, thus ushering in the era of the "new heavens and the new earth" (Rev. 21.1).

Spirituality of the last things

We live at a time when death is concealed from us in myriad ways and as a result the meaning and seriousness of life is obscured. We are increasingly alienated from our true selves, others, and God by the idols and illusions caused by over-attachment to the internet, television, video games, cell phones, our physical appearance, money, and many other things. It is important for us to make a concerted effort to live intentionally for God with our eyes firmly fixed on the things that truly matter. "Do not work for the food that perishes but for the food that endures for eternal life" (Jn 6.27). We should be neither preoccupied with death nor should we deny it. Teresa of Avila, in her *Spiritual Maxims*, exhorts us to "remember that you have only one soul; that you have only one death to die; that you have only one life. [. . .] If you do this, there will be many things about which you care nothing." The traditional practice of an annual *silent* retreat of three, five or eight days under the direction of a trusted spiritual guide can help center us on what is truly important.

In his Rule for monasteries, St Benedict wisely counsels monks "to keep death daily before one's eyes." Preparing for a so-called "happy death" means beginning to live a genuinely happy life. Jesus reminds us of the importance of always being prepared for his coming. In the parable of the ten bridesmaids (Mt. 25.1–13), five had oil in their lamps and five did not when the bridegroom—an image of Christ—arrived. Spiritual writers have seen in the oil an allusion to deifying grace and the divine indwelling. The importance of always being prepared to meet Christ is underscored in his words at the end of the parable: "Keep awake therefore, for you know neither the day nor the hour." As Pope John XXIII said on his deathbed: "My bags are packed and I am ready, very ready, to go."

Besides frequent participation in the Sacrament of Reconciliation or confession, the private renewal of our baptismal vows in which we make a more resolute renunciation of the devil, the world, sin, and our selfish selves so as to give ourselves entirely to Jesus can be helpful.

"That you may be filled with all the fullness of God"

"If God is for us, who is against us?" (Rom. 8.31) The fact that God is indeed on our side and desires to share his divine life with us is manifested in an indubitable way in the suffering and death of the God-Man, Jesus Christ, who said, "God did not send the Son into the world to condemn the world, but in order that the world might be saved through him" (Jn 3.17). Because we have received the gift of faith we believe that God desires more than anything else to fill us with all the fullness of his divine life, beginning in the present life and brought to fulfillment in the next.

In the light of glory we will see God as he is and for the first time we will also see ourselves in the fullness of our glorified humanity. We will be given a new name (Rev. 2.17) which will reflect our true identity as unique and precious images of Christ. Then we will spontaneously join the heavenly chorus in praising God, saying

Holy, Holy, Holy Lord God of hosts.
Heaven and earth are full of your glory.
Hosanna in the highest.

Blessed is he who comes in the name of the Lord.
Hosanna in the highest.

⬆

Prayer of St Albert the Great

O Lord Jesus Christ, the great householder, who from the first light of dawn has called me into the vineyard when you hired me from my youth to labor in religion for the denarius of eternal life. When, in judgment, evening is come and you give to the workmen their reward, what will you give to me who have stood the whole day of my life idle—not merely in the market place of the world but in the very vineyard of religion?

O Lord, who does not measure our works by their public value but by their eternal merit before you, at least in the eleventh hour change me

so that I may be found not entirely wanting in your sight. Amen.

Notes

1 Quoted in Peter van Breeman, SJ, *The God Who Won't Let Go* (Notre Dame, IN: Ave Maria Press, 2001), p. 146. No citation given.
2 CCC, 1024, 2794.
3 Pope Benedict XVI, "Encyclical on Hope," *Spe Salvi* (November 30, 2007), §10 at the Holy See, www.vatican.va.
4 CCC, 1720.
5 Catherine of Siena, *Dialogue* (trans. Noffke), ch. 100, p. 188.
6 Pope Benedict XVI, *Spe Salvi*, §12 quoted in Paul O'Callaghan, *Christ Our Hope. An Introduction to Eschatology* (Washington, DC: The Catholic University of America Press, 2011), p. 157.
7 Catherine of Siena, *Dialogue* (trans. Noffke), ch. 60, p. 115.
8 Augustine of Hippo, "Letter," 147, 37 in Augustine of Hippo, *The Works of Saint Augustine. A Translation for the 21st century. Letters 100–155* (II/2) (trans. with notes by Roland Teske; Hyde Park, NY: New City Press, 2003), p. 338.
9 Ps. 36.9.

10 Pope Benedict XII, *Benedictus Deus* (1336); DS 1000.
11 See 2 Kgs 6.17.
12 Catherine of Siena, *Dialogue* (trans. Noffke), ch. 96, p. 181.
13 See ibid., ch. 101, p. 192.
14 Innocenzo Colosio, OP, "La infinità del desiderio secondo S. Caterina da Siena," in *S. Caterina tra i dottori della Chiesa* (ed. Tito S. Centi, OP; Firenze: Casa Editrice A. Salani, 1970), p. 78.
15 Gregory of Nyssa, *Homilies on the Song of Songs*, 12; PG 44, 1036, quoted in Clément, *The Roots of Christian Mysticism*, p. 191.
16 Gregory of Nyssa, *Homilies on the Song of Songs*, 8; PG 44, 940–41, quoted in Clément, *The Roots of Christian Mysticism*, p. 240
17 Catherine of Siena, *Dialogue* (trans. Noffke), ch. 134, p. 273.
18 Bernard of Clairvaux, *On the Song of Songs*, Sermon 84, no. 1, quoted in Ralph Martin, *The Fulfillment of all Desire. A Guidebook for the Journey to God Based on the Wisdom of the Saints* (Steubenville, OH: Emmaus Road Publishing, 2006), pp. 188–89.
19 Catherine of Siena, *Dialogue* (trans. Noffke), ch. 41, p. 83.
20 Joseph Ratzinger, *Eschatology: Death and Eternal Life* (Washington, DC: Catholic University of America Press, 1988), p. 216.
21 CCC, 1035.
22 CCC, 1033. Italics mine.
23 Paul O'Callaghan, *Christ Our Hope. An Introduction to Eschatology* (Washington, DC: The Catholic University of America Press, 2011), p. 206.
24 Letter T348 in Catherine of Siena, *The Letters* (trans. Noffke; vol. 4), p. 167.
25 Isaac of Nineveh, *Ascetic Treatises*, 84 quoted in Clément, *The Roots of Christian Mysticism*, p. 302.
26 Pope St Gregory the Great, *Dialogue* 4, 41:3 quoted in O'Callaghan, *Christ Our Hope*, p. 291.

WORKS CITED

Ancilli, E. and D. de Pablo Maroto, "Caterina da Siena (santa)." In *Dizionario eniclopedico di spiritualità* (vol. 1; Nuova edizione; Roma: Città Nuova Editrice, 1990).

Arintero, John G., OP, *The Mystical Evolution in the Development and Vitality of the Church* (trans. Jordan Aumann, OP; 2 vols; St. Louis, MO: B. Herder, 1949).

Ashley, Benedict M., OP, *Living the Truth in Love. A biblical introduction to moral theology* (Staten Island, NY: Alba House, 1996).

Athanasius of Alexandria, *St. Athanasius on the Incarnation* (intro. C. S. Lewis; trans. Religious of the CSMV; Crestwood, NY: St. Vladimir's Seminary Press, 1993).

Augustine of Hippo, *Commentary on the Lord's Sermon on the Mount with Seventeen Related Sermons* (trans. Denis J. Kavanaugh, OSA; The Fathers of the Church. A New Translation; New York: Fathers of the Church, 1951).

—, *The Confessions of St. Augustine* (trans. F. J. Sheed; New York: Sheed & Ward, 1957).

—, *Expositions of the Psalms 33–50* (trans. Marie Boulding, OSB; The Works of Saint Augustine. A Translation for the 21st Century; Hyde Park: New City Press, 2000).

—, *Letters 100–155 (II/2)* (trans. Roland Teske; The Works of Saint Augustine. A translation for the 21st century; Hyde Park, NY: New City Press, 2003).

—, *On the Lord's Sermon on the Mount*. In *Nicene and Post-Nicene Fathers, First Series* (vol. 6. Buffalo, NY: Christian Literature Publishing Co., 1888).

—, *On the Trinity (De Trinitate)* (intro., trans., and notes by Edmund Hill, OP; The Works of St. Augustine; Hyde Park: New City Press, 2007).

—, *Soliloquies. Augustine's interior dialogue* (trans. and notes by Kim Paffenroth; The Augustine Series; Hyde Park: New City Press, 2000).

Aumann, Jordan, OP, *Spiritual Theology* (London: Sheed & Ward, 1980).

Budge, Ernest A. W., trans. *The Paradise or Garden of the Holy Fathers* (vol. 2; London: Catto & Windus, 1907).

Cantalamessa, Raniero, OFMCap, *The Eucharist, Our sanctification* (Collegeville, MN: Liturgical Press, 1993).

— *Catechism of the Catholic Church* (Washington, DC: United States Catholic Conference, 2nd edn, 2000).

Caterina da Siena, *Il Dialogo*. (*A cura di* G. Cavallini; Roma: Edizioni Cateriniane, 1968).

Catherine of Siena, *Catherine of Siena. The Dialogue* (trans. Suzanne Noffke, OP; The Classics of Western Spirituality; New York and Mahwah: Paulist Press, 1980).

—, *The Dialogue of the Seraphic Virgin Catherine of Siena* (trans. Algar Thorold; London: Kegan Paul, Trench, Trűbner, 1896).

—, *The Letters of Catherine of Siena* (trans. Suzanne Noffke, OP; 4 vols; Tempe, AZ: Arizona Center for Medieval and Renaissance Studies, 2000–2008).

—, *The Prayers of Catherine of Siena* (trans. Suzanne Noffke, OP; San Jose, CA: Authors Choice Press, 2nd edn, 2001).

Caussade, Jean-Pierre, *Abandonment to Divine Providence* (trans. J. Beevers; New York: Image, 1993).

Ciszek, Walter, SJ, *He Leadeth Me* (Garden City: Doubleday, 1973).

Clément, Olivier, *The Roots of Christian Mysticism. Texts from the patristic era with commentary* (New York: New City, 1995).

Colosio, Innocenzo, OP, "La infinità del desiderio secondo S. Caterina da Siena." In *S. Caterina tra i dottori della Chiesa* (ed. Tito S. Centi, OP; Firenze: Casa Editrice A. Salani, 1970), pp. 69–82

Cyprian of Carthage, *Treatises* (trans. and ed. Roy J. Deferrari; The Fathers of the Church. A New Translation; New York: Fathers of the Church, 1958).

Dubay, Thomas, SM, *God Dwells Within Us* (Denville, NJ: Dimension Books, 1971).

Eliot, T. S., *The Complete Poems and Plays 1909–1950* (New York: Harcourt, 1971).

Escrivá, Josemaria, *Friends of God: Homilies* (New York: Scepter, 2003).

Foster, Kenelm, OP, "St. Catherine's Teaching on Christ." In *Life of the Spirit* 16 (1962), pp. 310–23.

Garrigou-Lagrange, Reginald, OP, *Christian Perfection and Contemplation, According to St. Thomas Aquinas and St. John of the Cross* (trans. Sister M. Timothea Doyle; St. Louis; MO: B. Herder, 1937).

Green, Bernard D., SDS, *Christian Spirituality and Human Development. A philosophical and psychological inquiry* (Tempe, AZ: Institute for the Study of Catholic Faith and Life, 2009).

—, *Death, Sin and the Gospel* (Tempe, AZ: Institute for the Study of Catholic Faith and Life, 2006).

—, *The Humility of God. Reflections on the importance of the Trinity in Christian experience* (Tempe, AZ: Institute for the Study of Catholic Faith and Life, 2009).

Grion, Alvaro, OP, *La dottrina di Santa Caterina da Siena* (Brescia: Morcelliana, 1962).

Hardon, John, SJ, *History and Theology of Grace* (Ann Arbor, MI: Veritas Press, 2003).

Ignatius of Loyola, *The Spiritual Exercises of St. Ignatius of Loyola* (trans. Elder Mullan; New York: Kennedy, 1914).

Irenaeus of Lyons, *Against Heresies* (ed. Alexander Roberts, et al.; vol. 9; Ante-Nicene Christian Library; Edinburgh: T&T Clarke, 1869).

Jarrett, Bede, OP, *He Dwells in Your Soul* (Manchester, NH: Sophia Institute Press, 1998).

John Chrysostom, *The Homilies of S. John Chrysostom on the Epistles of St. Paul the Apostle to Timothy, Titus and Philemon* (trans. members of the English Church; Oxford: Parker, 1743).

John of the Cross, *The Collected Works of St. John of the Cross* (trans. Kieran Kavanaugh, OCD, and Otilio Rodriguez, OCD; Washington, DC: Institute of Carmelite Studies, 1991).

Leen, Edward, CSSp, *Progress Through Mental Prayer* (New York: Sheed & Ward, 1935).

Lewis, C. S., *Mere Christianity* (London: Macmillan, 1958).

Lossky, Vladimir, *The Mystical Theology of the Eastern Church* (Crestwood, NY: St. Vladimir's Seminary Press, 1976).

Marmion, Columba, OSB, *Christ in His Mysteries* (new trans. Alan Bancroft; Bethesda, MD: Zaccheus Press, 2008).

—, *Christ the Life of the Soul* (St. Louis, MO: B. Herder, 1925).

McCabe, Herbert, OP, *God, Christ and Us* (New York: Continuum, 2005).

—, *Teaching of the Catholic Church* (London: Darton, Logmann & Todd, 2000).

McGinn, Bernard, "Mysticism." In *The New Westminster Dictionary of Christian Spirituality* (ed. Philip Sheldrake; Louisville, KY: Westminster John Knox Press, 2005).

Meconi, David V., SJ, "Deification in the Thought of John Paul II," *Irish Theological Quarterly*, 2006, pp. 127–41.

Mitchell, W. and the Carisbrooke Dominicans, trans. *Christian Asceticism and Modern Man* (New York: Philosophical Library, 1955).

Moynihan, Anselm, OP, *The Presence of God* (Dublin: St. Martin Apostolate, 1948).

Newman, John Henry, *Parochial and Plain Sermons* (vol. 1; London: Rivington, 1879).

O'Callaghan, Paul, *Christ Our Hope. An Introduction to Eschatology* (Washington, DC: The Catholic University of America Press, 2011).

Philippe, Jacques, *Interior Freedom* (New York: Scepter, 2007).

—, *Time for God* (New York: Scepter, 2008).

Pope Benedict XVI, Angelus (May 31, 2009). At the Holy See, www.vatican.va.

—, "Encyclical on Hope," *Spe salvi* (November 30, 2007). At the Holy See, www.vatican.va.

—, "Encyclical on the Love of God," *Deus Caritas est* (December 25, 2005). At the Holy See, www.vatican.va.

—, "Question and Answer Session with Priests at the End of the Year of the Priest" (June 10, 2010). At the Holy See, www.vatican.va.

Pope John Paul II, (Papa Giovanni Paolo II), Angelus (julio 1, 1999). At the Holy See, www.vatican.va.

—, Apostolic Letter, *Novo Millennio Ineunte* (January 6, 2001). At the Holy See, www.vatican.va.

—, Apostolic Letter, *Rosarium Virginis Mariae* (October 16, 2002). At the Holy See, www.vatican.va.

—, *Go in Peace. A Gift of Enduring Love* (Chicago, IL: University of Loyola Press, 2005).

Ratzinger, Joseph [later Pope Benedict XVI], *Eschatology: Death and Eternal Life* (Washington, DC: The Catholic University of America Press, 1988).

Ratzinger, Joseph [Pope Benedict XVI], *Jesus of Nazareth: From the Baptism in the Jordan to the Transfiguration* (San Francisco, CA: Ignatius Press, 2008).

Raymond of Capua, *The Life of Catherine of Siena* (trans. Conleth Kearns, OP; Wilmington, DE: Michael Glazier, 1980).

Rolheiser, Ronald, *The Holy Longing. The Search for a Christian Spirituality* (New York: Image Doubleday, 1999).

Sayers, Dorothy L. *The Greatest Drama Ever Staged* (London: Hodder & Stoughton, 1938).

Second Vatican Council, "The Constitution on the Sacred Liturgy," *Sacrosanctum Concilium* (December 4, 1963). In *Vatican Council II. The Conciliar and Post Conciliar Documents* (ed. Austin Flannery, OP; vol. 1; Northport, NY: Costello, 1975), pp. 1–270.

—, "Declaration on the Relation of the Church to Non-Christian Religions," *Nostra Aetate* (October 28, 1965). In *Vatican Council II. The Conciliar and Post Conciliar Documents* (ed. Austin Flannery, OP; vol. 1; 1988 rev. edn; Northport, NY: Costello, 1975), pp. 738–49.

Second Vatican Council, "Pastoral Constitution on the Church in the Modern World," *Gaudium et Spes* (December 7, 1965). In *Vatican Council II. The Conciliar and Post Conciliar Documents* (ed. Austin Flannery, OP; vol. 1; Northport, NY: Costello, 1975), pp. 903–1014.

—, "Dogmatic Constitution on the Church," *Lumen Gentium* (November 21, 1964). In *Vatican Council II. The Conciliar and Post Conciliar Documents* (ed. Austin Flannery, OP; vol. 1; Northport, NY: Costello, 1975), pp. 350–432.

Sheed, F. J., *Theology and Sanity* (London: Sheed and Ward, 1978).

Teresa, Mother, *Come Be My Light. The Private Writings of the "Saint of Calcutta,"* (ed. Brian Kolodiejchuk, MC; New York: Image Doubleday, 2007).

Teresa of Avila, *The Complete Works of Saint Teresa of Avila* (trans. E. Allison Peers; London: Sheed & Ward, 1950).

—, *The Collected Works of St. Teresa of Avila* (trans. Kevin Kavanaugh and Otilio Rodriguez; 2 vols; Washington, DC: Institute of Carmelite Studies, 1976–80).

Thérèse of Lisieux, *St. Thérèse of Lisieux. Her Last Conversations* (trans. John Clarke, OCD; Washington, DC: Institute of Carmelite Studies, 1977).

—, *Story of a Soul. The Autobiography of St. Thérèse of Lisieux* (trans. John Clarke, OCD; Washington, DC: Institute of Carmelite Studies, 3rd edn, 1996.

Thomas à Kempis, *The Imitation of Christ* (trans. William C. Creasy; Notre Dame, IN: Ave Maria Press, 1989).

Thomas Aquinas, *Summa Theologica* (trans. Fathers of the English Dominican Province; New York: Benziger, 1947–48).

van Breeman, Peter, SJ, *The God Who Won't Let Go* (Notre Dame, IN: Ave Maria Press, 2001).

William of Saint Thierry, *On Contemplating God; Prayer; Meditations* (trans. Penelope Lawson, CSMV; Cistercian Fathers Series Number 3; Kalamazoo, MI: Cistercian Publications, 1970).

INDEX